D1278676

Kids InSight

Reconsidering How to Meet the Literacy Needs of All Students

Deborah R. Dillon
Purdue University
West Lafayette, Indiana, USA

INTERNATIONAL Reading Association

800 Barksdale Road, PO Box 8139
Newark, Delaware 19714-8139, USA
www.reading.org

IRA BOARD OF DIRECTORS

Carol Minnick Santa, School District #5, Kalispell, Montana, *President* • Carmelita K. Williams, Norfolk State University, Norfolk, Virginia, *President-Elect* • Donna Ogle, National-Louis University, Evanston, Illinois, *Vice President* • Kathryn H. Au, University of Hawaii, Honolulu, Hawaii • Betsy M. Baker, Columbia Public Schools, Columbia, Missouri • Patricia A. Edwards, Michigan State University, East Lansing, Michigan • Adria F. Klein, California State University, San Bernardino, California • Gregg M. Kurek, F.C. Reed Middle School, Bridgman, Michigan • Diane L. Larson, Owatonna Public Schools, Owatonna, Minnesota • Jeanne R. Paratore, Boston University, Boston, Massachusetts • Lori L. Rog, Regina Public School Board, Regina, Saskatchewan, Canada • Timothy Shanahan, University of Illinois at Chicago, Chicago, Illinois • Alan E. Farstrup, Executive Director

The International Reading Association attempts, through its publications, to provide a forum for a wide spectrum of opinions on reading. This policy permits divergent viewpoints without implying the endorsement of the Association.

Director of Publications   Joan M. Irwin
Assistant Director of Publications   Jeanette K. Moss
Editor in Chief, Books   Matthew W. Baker
Permissions Editor   Janet S. Parrack
Associate Editor   Tori Mello
Publications Coordinator   Beth Doughty
Association Editor   David K. Roberts
Production Department Manager   Iona Sauscermen
Art Director   Boni Nash
Senior Electronic Publishing Specialist   Anette Schütz-Ruff
Electronic Publishing Specialist   Cheryl J. Strum
Electronic Publishing Assistant   Jeanine K. McGann

Project Editor   Matthew W. Baker

Photo credits   Cover, Comstock Stock Photography

Copyright 2000 by the International Reading Association, Inc.
All rights reserved. No part of this publication may be reproduced or transmitted in any form or by any means, electronic or mechanical, including photocopy, or any informational storage and retrieval system, without permission from the publisher.

Library of Congress Cataloging in Publication Data
Dillon, Deborah R.
  Kids InSight : reconsidering how to meet the literacy needs of all students / Deborah R. Dillon.
      p. cm. -- (Kids InSight series)
  Includes bibliographical references and index.
  ISBN 0-87207-265-7
  1. Language arts (Secondary)--United States--Case studies. 2. Effective teaching--United States--Case studies. I. Title. II. Series.
LB1631 .D52 2000
373.1102--dc21   00-035103

Second Printing, November 2002

Kit
LB
1574.5
.A6
2002
pt.3

Dedication

Many of you may have seen the movie *The Joy Luck Club* (re-leased in 1993, novel written by Amy Tan, 1989), a story of four Chinese women who came to the United States many years ago and their daughters who grew up Chinese American. The women formed a strong friendship and the story relates the various difficulties and tragedies in each mother's life, in the relationships between the four mothers and daughters, and in each daughter's life. In a scene in the movie, one daughter named June talks with her mother about how sorry she is that she hasn't been the high-quality daughter her mother might have wished for; she also regrets the fact that her mother doesn't really see her for who she is.

June: I'm just sorry that you got stuck with such a loser...my grades...everything you expected of me.

Su Yuan (mother): Never expect. Only hope! Only hoping best for you.

June: No matter what you hope for, I'll never be more than what I am. And you never see that, what I really am.

(Su Yuan takes June's face in her hands and softly yet emotionally cries out "I SEE YOU. I SEE YOU.")

Su Yuan: That bad crab [a broken crab served at a dinner party that evening] only you tried to take it. Everybody else want best quality. You, your thinking different...you took worst because you have best quality heart. You have style no one can teach. Must be born this way.

This exchange between a mother and daughter reminds me of myself as a young woman, of my mother, of future events with my daughter, and of what I need to remember as a teacher: It is important for educators to really see who students are—as individual human beings and learners. And we must not only hope for the best where students are concerned, rather, we must support learners as they grow and develop into the best that they can be—individuals with quality hearts and minds, appreciated for their special talents, contributions, and "style."

In light of this message, I dedicate this book to the diversity of learners in our world and all the teachers who care so deeply about them. As we teach, may our thinking be "different" and may we "see" what is truly important in each learner.

Contents

Kids InSight Review Board

Jo Beth Allen
University of Georgia
Athens, Georgia, USA

Deanna Birdyshaw
Michigan Department of
    Education
Lansing, Michigan, USA

Fenice B. Boyd
University of Georgia
Athens, Georgia, USA

Faye Brownlie
Vancouver, British Columbia,
    Canada

Brenda Church
Akron Public Schools
Akron, Ohio, USA

Richard C. Culyer
Coker College
Hartsville, South Carolina, USA

H. Gay Fawcett
Summit County Education
    Service Center
Cuyahoga Falls, Ohio, USA

Robert Fecho
University of Georgia
Athens, Georgia, USA

Lee Galda
University of Minnesota
Minneapolis, Minnesota, USA

William A. Henk
Penn State University
Middletown, Pennsylvania, USA

Gay Ivey
University of Maryland
College Park, Maryland, USA

Sharon Arthur Moore
Peoria Unified School District #11
Glendale, Arizona, USA

David G. O'Brien
Purdue University
West Lafayette, Indiana, USA

Lisa Cross Stanzi
David C. Barrow Elementary
Athens, Georgia, USA

Melvin L. Thursby
Prairie Middle School
Cedar Rapids, Iowa, USA

Jan Turbill
University of Wollongong
Wollongong, New South Wales,
    Australia

Angela Ward
University of Saskatchewan
Saskatoon, Saskatchewan,
    Canada

Deborah A. Wooten
Glenwood Landing School
Glen Head, New York, USA

Josephine P. Young
Arizona State University
Tempe, Arizona, USA

Acknowledgments

I want to acknowledge the many individuals who contributed to the conceptualization of the Kids InSight series as well as to the ideas and effort reflected in this particular book. First, my thanks go to Joan Irwin, Director of Publications at the International Reading Association, and to Lee Gunderson and members of the IRA Publications Committee, who conceptualized the Kids InSight series several years ago. These individuals supported my debut as the first Series Editor and patiently waited as I recuperated from an illness that prevented me from moving forward with their ideas at that time. Thanks also go to Matt Baker, IRA Editor in Chief–Books, and his excellent staff who have helped to edit and format the Kids InSight books so that they appeal to readers and portray ideas clearly. Thanks also go to Beth Doughty for her efforts and those of the Kids InSight Review Board who reviewed this book and others and continue to offer ways to make the series of high quality.

Second, my efforts were enhanced through conversations and interactions I had with Elizabeth Moje, Lee Galda, Shane Rayburn, and Lisa Stanzi, authors of the first two books in the Kids InSight series that follow this foundational text. I appreciate their willingness to be my friend yet my colleague as we worked together to create our books and offered each other constructive feedback.

Third, I would be remiss if I didn't thank my wonderful family who supported me as I worked on this writing project. My parents, sisters and their families, and my professional colleagues are to be commended for their patience with me as I devoted my efforts to writing and potentially neglected other important activities. My appreciation and love for my husband and colleague, David O'Brien, also grew as I worked on this book. He provided valuable feedback on drafts of my manuscript and cared for our daughter, Erin Margaret, who patiently waited for mommy to "stop working and come up out of the basement and play with me!" I must confess that I am happy to have emerged from the basement.

And finally, I want to thank all of the students and teachers I have closely interacted with over the years. Many of these individuals are described in this book and they continue to be an inspiration to me as a teacher. I also want to thank each of you—the readers of this book. I learned a lot by writing this text and I hope you find meaning in my message as well.

Introduction

The Kids InSight Series:
Teachers Learning From Learners

Kids InSight is a book series that provides practical information for K–12 teachers and brings to the fore stories about children and adolescents as the basis for instructional decisions. The series title has a dual meaning: As educators, we must keep students foremost *in sight* as we think about and design literacy learning experiences, and we gain a great deal of *insight* about learning processes as we listen to and watch students. By listening to, watching, and talking to students; examining our beliefs and practices; and updating our literacy knowledge base, we can work toward the goal of meeting the literacy needs of the learners in our classrooms.

The primary audience for the Kids InSight series is classroom teachers; however, the books will be useful to college and university faculty working with preservice and inservice teachers, and to individuals in other educational settings. The books in the series will encourage these educators to address the challenge of meeting students' needs. All the authors in this series emphasize that there are no easy answers or quick fixes to achieving the goal of meeting learners' needs. However, by engaging in inquiry, reflection, and dialogue with others over time, we can learn ways to examine, think about, and reconsider our practices as we move forward in our professional development.

The process described in the preceding paragraph *is not* a process of reforming our work as teachers, a process predicated on the need for large-scale efforts to reformulate or restructure what we do because

1

everything is in need of change. Rather, the process is one of *renewal*, described by educational researcher Gary Fenstermacher (1999) as, "capitalizing on the strengths of what is already in place, while also acknowledging the challenges facing those who populate the organization undergoing renewal" (p. 8). In the Kids InSight series the goal is for teachers to reflect on and reconsider what we already do, change our focus to our students, view learners' actions in light of new data, and renew our teaching efforts.

Features of the Kids InSight Series

Important ideas or threads run throughout books in the series, linking one set of ideas to another within each book, and connecting each book to others in the series. The first feature is the style that authors use when writing their message. Each writer offers conversations in which the complexities of literacy teaching and learning are explored, and presents teachers working toward a new vision of meeting all students' literacy needs.

A second feature of the series is a focus on tensions and complexities that most teachers encounter in their daily work and as they engage in the process of renewal. Authors will identify and discuss these tensions and consider how they provide opportunities for educators to reflect on and reconsider their own practices in light of new knowledge about individual learners, literacy processes, and classroom practices.

To illuminate the tensions faced by educators and to illustrate particular teaching and learning moments, series authors will open each chapter with stories from teachers and learners and use these throughout the books. This third feature of the series—actual data clips that reveal students' and teachers perspectives—will provide glimpses into classrooms or reflection journals and present individual students from across the world, describing their lives in and out of classrooms. Stories, excerpts from classroom lessons, and interviews allow us to see how teachers and students think and work individually and collectively toward literacy learning, and let us examine the strategies teachers use to carefully listen to and observe learners.

A fourth feature of the series is the use of a sociocultural-cognitive perspective of how children learn and develop as literate individuals. We are familiar with the literature that outlines how children learn from a cognitive perspective; specifically, children are active, constructive learners who work to interpret and make sense of their world based on what they already know and what they construct or reconstruct as they participate in experiences or glean new information. Children also construct knowledge through the use of language—this is how meanings are expressed and communicated. Language is used in multiple ways with different patterns that occur as we interact with others in various social contexts. Learning, then, is a social activity that influences and is influenced by our culture, the social situations in which we find ourselves, and the interactions we have with particular people—all of which occur at various points in our lives. The sociocultural-cognitive perspective of learning, described in more detail later in this book, undergirds the series and provides a consistent philosophy of learning and teaching across the books.

A fifth feature of the series is a focus on the emotional development of learners. This perspective reminds us that a learner's cognitive and social learning are impacted by their emotions about themselves, peers, teachers, and the learning situation. The classroom environments we design for learners must be safe and yet offer other conditions that support learning and motivate students to want to learn in meaningful ways. Further, series authors recognize that as educators we must take a critical stance on what occurs in and out of our classrooms. Specifically, we must challenge ourselves and students to question long-held beliefs, and we must change actions that do not support the learning or emotional development of all individuals, regardless of a person's race, cultural or social background, or cognitive abilities.

A sixth feature of the series is a commitment by authors to document various literacy events and practices and detail the planning and implementation of literacy activities and programs. Authors will describe sample lessons designed for particular students or groups of students, and will highlight examples of students' multiple literacies. Materials and lists of resources to adapt and use when designing curricula also will be provided. Teachers will discuss how they created new programs, the challenges and tensions that emerged as teachers and students implemented new ideas, what worked or did not work and why, and the learning of children as a result of new programs designed to meet their needs.

Finally, Reflection Points can be found throughout each book. This special feature will allow educators to individually engage in professional development and form collaborative inquiry groups within their school or district; in these groups colleagues can read, write, talk about, implement, and reflect on new ideas. Specifically, teachers are asked to stop periodically throughout each book to engage in activities such as the following:

- Reflect on and write about your current teaching practices, including the tensions or dilemmas that arise daily related to learners, learning and teaching, and reflect on new knowledge associated with meeting all students' literacy needs (such as current literacy research supporting effective classroom practices).

- Collect other forms of data, such as artifacts of students' learning and questionnaires and interviews with students, which provide information about learners, teaching, and learning processes.

- Analyze multiple data sources, focusing on understanding your literacy beliefs and practices and the beliefs, interests, and needs of your students.

- Read literacy research related to questions that arise for you after reflecting, collecting, and analyzing data, and think about how findings have been translated into effective literacy practices by K–12 teachers and students. Compare your interpretations and responses to the research literature with peers.

- Reconsider current practices and entertain new possibilities.

- Reconceptualize ideas about literacy learning, teaching, and assessment.

- Construct a renewed vision based on the needs of particular students.

Let's Get Started

Before we move on to Chapter 1, I invite you to purchase a journal or create one where you can write responses to Reflection Points presented throughout books in the series, and where you can record other ideas you generate. Next, I urge you to set aside small blocks of quiet time—perhaps during lunch or before or after school. Record the questions posed in Reflection Points throughout books in the series in your journal and then free write a response, unencumbered by worries about how your thoughts sound or look. Peter Elbow (1998) in his book *Writing Without Teachers* presents the idea of free writing as a technique writers can use when they are a bit threatened by an assignment or new materials or encounter some form of writer's block. When we free write we think about the topic for a short time and then write without stopping or thinking about what will come next. The goal is to get as many ideas down on paper as possible, expressing thoughts honestly and completely. As Kirby, Liner, and Vinz (1981) note, "Getting it right comes from getting it down" (p. 16). Reflections of this sort make the analysis and interpretation process richer and more meaningful. It is also important to set aside time for reflecting on what your responses mean and gathering information and data to make your professional development process richer.

Finally, readers may choose to read Kids InSight books on their own while others may want to form inquiry groups or study groups. This latter arrangement has been found to be very powerful in supporting individual professional development as well as allowing some interesting and meaningful dialogue across various grades and schools within a district.

As you continue to read this book and others in the Kids InSight series, I invite you to join with the authors as we think about how to create exciting, meaningful classrooms where teachers and students learn and feel a great deal of satisfaction with their efforts.

Chapter 1

Keeping Students in Sight
to Glean Insights

I just finished rereading Crow Boy *by Taro Yashima (1955). This is the story of a young man named Chibi and his life in school, grades 1 through 6. His classmates and teachers considered Chibi strange. He was afraid of the other children and appeared unable to learn anything. No one worked with Chibi during class or played with him at recess. In fact, other kids began calling Chibi "stupid" and "slowpoke." Chibi began to act out in class and seek ways to entertain himself, eventually escaping to an inner world. Just before Chibi's sixth (and last) year in school, a new teacher, Mr. Isobe, was hired to teach sixth grade and he decided to learn everything he could about Chibi. Mr. Isobe found out that Chibi knew about plants and gardening, and that he could represent his ideas in drawings and writings, some of which only Chibi could read and understand. The sixth grade had a talent show and all the students were stunned when Chibi appeared. Chibi stood on the stage and imitated the voices of newly hatched crows and their mother, crows in the morning and at night, and happy and sad crows. Chibi's performance was very effective. The audience members were able to imagine where the crows lived and where Chibi lived with his family. At this point in the story the author writes,*

Then Mr. Isobe explained how Chibi had learned those calls—leaving his home for school at dawn, and arriving home at sunset, everyday for six long years. Every one of us cried, thinking how much we had been wrong to Chibi all those long years. Even grown-ups wiped their eyes, saying, "Yes, yes he is wonderful." Soon after that came

graduation day. Chibi was the only one in our class honored for perfect attendance through all the six years.

The story concludes with Chibi—now referred to as "Crow Boy"
by everyone—happily working to make life better for his family and
being respected by those who live in the village.

Deborah Dillon

The story *Crow Boy* is set in Japan, but the message is universal.
Every time I read this book I get a lump in my throat. I am reminded of what is most important in the lives of teachers like you
and me—the individual students we teach each day, every year. But how
do we keep learners like Chibi "in sight," first and foremost, as we deal
with the complexities of education and design meaningful learning experiences? How do we meet the literacy needs of all students? Addressing questions like these is a goal of this book, the first in the Kids InSight
series. What follows is the first Reflection Point of the series. Please write
these questions and your responses in your journal. In the next section
of the chapter I offer detailed ideas and examples on the process of reflecting and analyzing your thoughts.

Reflection Point

Describe a student you have taught that reminds you of Chibi.
What strategies have you used to help you keep individual students like Chibi "in sight," or to glean insights about the various
learners in your classroom?

Strategies for Analyzing Reflections

Reflecting and writing down thoughts is an important first step in
thinking about learners and examining one's instructional beliefs and
practices. We will revisit this idea several times throughout this book be-

cause learning to analyze what our thoughts may mean is key to thinking about our practices. Here is a strategy I have used with colleagues as we have sought to understand our ideas: Take a piece of paper and create a data analysis worksheet. Make two columns at the top of the page, labeling one "What I seem to be saying" and the second column "What my thoughts seem to mean." Reread your response to the first question. In the left-hand column, summarize or describe the key ideas from your response, using actual words in this brief description (this practice keeps your analysis very close to the original data source). Follow this same process when you analyze the second question. Next, consider what your responses and summary analyses seem to mean. In other words, what do your responses tell you about yourself as a teacher? About the students you work with? About the classroom you teach in and the concerns you have as an educator? Write your analysis comments in the right-hand column across from the responses listed for questions one and two, respectively.

See Appendix A on page 157 for an example of my responses to the Reflection Point on page 7 and my analysis and interpretation of my comments. You may want to engage in your own analysis and then compare your findings and process with mine (there is not one "right" way to analyze data), or you may wish to read the example provided and conduct your own analysis. In either case, your goal is to glean insights about students and yourself.

An additional way to glean insights about individual learners involves collecting some informal data at the start of the school year or new semester. In Box 1-1 I provide a quick writing activity, the Autobiopoem, which I use each semester to learn about my individual students' interests, fears, and dreams. Student writing provides another data source that we can use to shape teaching and learning practices in our classrooms. Note what can be gleaned from a student's Autobiopoem, which follows the general poem format.

Who Am I and Why Am I Writing This Book?

Part of my reason for writing the foundation book in the Kids InSight series stems from who I am and my professional goals. I am first and foremost a teacher. In my role as a professor at the university level, I work with

---

BOX 1-1
Example of an Autobiopoem

Format for Poem
First Name
Four personal traits that describe you
Sibling of
Lover of (3 people or ideas)
Who feels (3 items)
Who needs (3 items)
Who gives (3 items)
Who fears (3 items)
Who would like to see (3 items)
Resident of (town or city, street)
Last name

Darin's Poem
Darin
Dumb, weird, spaced off, crazy
Brother of Todd and Michele
Lover of cute girls, fudge, chips, dip, pie
Who feels dumb, tired, happy
Who needs money, love, friends
Who gives happiness, rowdiness, help
Who fears death, jail, crazy people
Who would like to see World's of Fun, Canada, Europe
Resident of 100 Kenilworth Street
Waverly, Nebraska

Poem provided by a professor at the University of Nebraska

---

prospective and practicing teachers as we collaboratively learn about how students read, write, and use and develop language abilities. We also explore the roles we assume in helping students learn. I am also a researcher who enjoys collaborating with school-based and university colleagues as well as community members and parents to understand the complexities of learning and teaching. I recently became a parent for the first time, and in this role I have drawn from my skills as a teacher and researcher to support the learning and emotional needs of my daughter.

After earning a degree in K–12 music and elementary education, I started my teaching career in Waverly, Nebraska, where I taught elementary students in a rural school district. My desire to continue my education stemmed from my interactions with several fifth graders in my first year of teaching at Waverly Elementary School (one of these students, Darin, is discussed in my responses to Reflection Points in Appendix A). These students I was most challenged by—half my class of 20—had been identified as having reading problems. I struggled to figure out what these problems were, to determine ways to meet the students' learning and emotional needs, and to select materials and create activities to motivate these children. As a first-year teacher, I began to realize that teaching was much more complex than I had realized, and to avoid sinking into a pool of fear and insecurity, I took graduate courses in reading to add to my knowledge base about students' literacy development. It would be fair to say that my first few years of teaching were filled with experimenting, adjusting, discarding ideas, and surviving. Actually, all my years of teaching could be characterized in this manner; each day I think about the students in my classroom and my interactions with them, and I worry that I am not meeting their needs as learners.

After teaching several years in the public schools and earning a master's degree, I left Nebraska to work on a doctorate in reading education at the University of Georgia. During this time period I worked with adult learners who needed support in the areas of reading and writing, and I helped prepare preservice literacy teachers. I also worked on several grant projects that taught me the value of long-term collaborative research between university and school-based researchers. Specifically, I learned valuable lessons about how to observe and listen to students and teachers during classroom interactions. I learned about the roles that administrators and parents play in the learning process, and how the lives of teachers and students within and beyond school walls affect learning.

Goals to Achieve as We Seek to Meet the Needs of All Learners

My first goal in writing this book is based on my ongoing desire to learn more about what it means to be an effective teacher and to support others as they also seek to meet the needs of learners. Key to this goal is repositioning the role of the learner in the teaching-learning process. I was prepared as a teacher to think about selecting the best methods, the most appropriate skills and strategies, and useful materials to use with my students. As I interacted with students, I focused my attention on my actions as a teacher, working to become more effective in how I presented information, assessed learning, and managed the classroom. I pitched my instruction to the class as a whole. In fact, I usually talked about my students as "my class." Because I focused on myself, the materials, skills and methods, and my class as a unit, I did not see the actions or interactions of individual students. I often was not aware of what one student knew or did not know, what particular children were interested in and what materials matched their interests and were challenging, or the most appropriate strategies to use to support an individual student's learning. I still struggle with this issue; it's not that I was (or am) a bad teacher, but I often do not pay attention to the key sources of information I need to guide my pedagogy—the individual learners in my classroom. This lack of focus on individual students became a tension for me—an incongruence between my vision and beliefs about learning processes, my role as a teacher, and my instructional practices.

Second, I have observed and worked with many students labeled as "struggling" or "at risk" who require the best learning opportunities that teachers can offer. These students may enter school from diverse cultural, social, and economic backgrounds; with limited English proficiency; with learning challenges; and from a variety of literacy and life experiences. These students are often not getting the support or experiences in school that they need to help them grow as learners and individuals. Instead, many students I have talked with feel disconnected from teachers and school, and have little desire to learn. Likewise, my conversations with teachers often center on their concern about particular learners and what they can do to engage students they "worry about" (Allen,

Michalove, Shockley, & West, 1991). Thus, a goal in writing this book is to think about ways to understand learners as individual people who are from diverse cultural backgrounds and are at various developmental levels, and who have different emotional issues in their lives.

My third goal is to work collaboratively with other educators to meet the needs of all students in all classrooms and schools, and to encourage teachers to work together as well. Research strongly indicates that if we are going to move forward in school renewal and in meeting all students' needs, we must focus on individuals as well as school and district-level professional development efforts. Students move from one teacher to another, year after year. It is not enough for a learner to have good experiences every few years in school. Rather, students require consistent, coherent, quality experiences each year, in every class and content area, to support their development.

All of the aforementioned goals are more important to me than ever before, because, as I mentioned previously, I recently became a mother. My husband and I adopted a baby girl from China named Erin. In one short year she has grown from a 13-month-old baby, who did not understand or speak any English, to a 2-year-old who continually seeks to communicate with and influence the actions of others to get what she wants and to understand the world around her. Like any parent, I want Erin to interact with knowledgeable teachers who appreciate her talents, care about her as a person, support her learning, and encourage within her a lifelong love of reading, writing, and learning. All my life I have focused on the goal of educating teachers to work with other people's children, recognizing that some teachers are more skilled than others. Currently, I am rededicating myself to the goal of supporting all teachers to be highly skilled professionals, because one of these individuals could be my daughter's teacher.

Reflection Point

Reflect on and write about your strengths as a teacher. What challenges do you face as you seek to meet the needs of all learners? What goals do you have for your future professional development?

Who Are the Teachers and Learners in This Book?

During my teaching career I have had the pleasure of collaborating with many outstanding educators in K–12 settings. The stories of these teachers and the learners in their classrooms are shared in this book. These stories serve to illuminate and inspire as well as present the complexities many of us face as we teach. This section will introduce you to several teachers and learners, describe the school settings and subject areas you will be reading about, and give you a sense of who these individuals are as people.

While at the University of Georgia I met an outstanding high school teacher named Rick Umpleby. Rick taught students at Brown-Hill High School, a seventh- to twelfth-grade facility in rural Georgia with a student population that was 74% Black and 26% White. The school is located in a community of approximately 13,000 people; at the time of the study only 32% of the parents in the community had graduated from high school and only 16% of these individuals attended college. Learners at the school were tracked into advanced, general, and basic classes early in their academic careers. To graduate, students had to pass a basic skills test (BST) in math and reading.

I spent a year in Rick's low-track English/reading classroom, observing and talking with him and his students. My research goal was to study the actions of the teacher and students in this classroom and understand how Rick created a learning environment that supported the cognitive and affective learning of students identified as low track—the students most people had given up on. Rick is a White man who was born and raised in Rochester, New York. He was 38 years old at the time of the study. Rick requested to work with the low-track students, and he was considered by students, parents, and administrators to be highly effective as a teacher and a coach. His students generally attended his classes and earned passing grades. They also participated in his class much more than they did in other classes and seemed to enjoy the reading and writing activities he designed to support their learning.

Of the 17 students I observed in Rick's classroom, most were African American. Ten of the students were females and seven were males, and most were in Grade 11. The students were from a variety of family structures and backgrounds, and two female students had children of their own. In this book you will meet several of these students, including Yvonne, an African American who lived with her grandmother and uncle in a very poor part of town. Yvonne valued education and wanted to graduate and attend a trade school where she could learn to work with computers. However, it appeared that despite her efforts to make money working outside school hours, it would be a tremendous challenge for her to earn the money she needed to further her education.

When I moved from Georgia to Lafayette, Indiana, I met Joe Ruhl, a high school biology teacher at Jefferson High School, a school with approximately 2,200 students. The school is located in an urban community with a population of more than 120,000 people from a wide cross-section of socioeconomic levels. The school had consisted primarily of White students; however, a recent influx of Hispanic families in the area has changed the racial composition. At the time of the study, students were tracked into advanced, general, and basic classes early in their academic careers.

My colleague, David O'Brien, and I spent a year in Joe's class, which consisted primarily of academic-track students. We audiotaped and videotaped lessons and formed a collaborative research agenda with Joe. We studied the social organization of the classroom, students' discourse during cooperative group sessions, their interactions with Joe and each other, and peer and teacher-student relationships that supported learning. Joe, in his mid-30s at the time of the study, is a White man with many years of teaching experience. He earned a master's degree in science education and has been awarded numerous local and national teaching honors including a presidential award for science and mathematics. Joe has a reputation in the school district as an outstanding teacher. Students want to be in his classes because they hear that sessions are fun and interesting, and that they promote successful learning. He is known as a caring teacher who believes that students need to understand how science affects their lives and how to make informed decisions based on an understanding of science and its impact on society.

David O'Brien and I attended one section of Joe's biology class each day for a year. The spring semester group of students consisted of 25 academic-track students, including 14 females and 11 males. All students in the class were White. Students were primarily tenth graders from a variety of socioeconomic backgrounds and ability levels.

In Joe's classroom I spent time interviewing and observing one group of five students who worked together during groupwork. One student I learned a great deal about was Carolyn. Carolyn grew up in a middle-class family, and after her parents divorced she decided to live with her mother. Carolyn's goal was to become a veterinarian. This caused her to view biology class as important and she worried about getting good grades. However, she also enjoyed attending school because of the many social opportunities available. She particularly enjoyed Joe's class because he allowed students to work on assignments in small groups and because he supported students' learning.

In addition to the two research studies outlined in this section, over the past 3 years I have engaged in long-term staff development with groups of K–5, middle school, and high school teachers in the Lafayette, Indiana area. These educators are interested in learning about literacy processes and reconsidering their practices as individuals and as team members within schools and across the district. Data from Rick Umpleby's and Joe Ruhl's classrooms, reflections from both teachers during research meetings, interviews with Rick's and Joe's students, and other data from Lafayette teachers will be evident in this book. I use these data because I admire these teachers and their work with students. I also have learned a great deal from my school-based colleagues that has positively influenced my teaching. I believe you will appreciate their struggles and triumphs as well.

Rick Umpleby and Joe Ruhl have taught me that meeting individual learners' needs requires new visions of teaching and learning, new ways to examine who students are and what they know, and new ways to interact with students. It requires new knowledge and beliefs about learners and teaching, and new practices in our classrooms. Developing these new knowledge bases will allow us to gain insights about our students and, in the process, to become insightful teachers who make a difference in the lives of learners. Insightfulness is a key characteristic of effective literacy teachers. We will begin to explore what it means to be insightful in the following section of this chapter.

Before we move on, you will note that I present the words of the teachers and students as true to form as I heard or received them. For example, I have not changed the grammar or spellings used by students and the teachers in transcripts and writings respectively. My intent is not to present natural language to display errors; rather, I want to preserve the oral language, dialects, and authentic writings shared with me. I believe this authenticity allows my audience to learn who the students and teachers are as individuals, as well as what they think and do on a daily basis. Likewise, the names of teachers and students have not been changed with the exception of the names of students in Rick Umpleby's classroom.

What Does It Mean to Be Insightful?

Webster's Dictionary (1979) defines *insight* as "the power or act of seeing into a situation; the act or result of apprehending the inner nature of things or seeing intuitively" (p. 592). Elliott Eisner (1991) builds on this idea in his book *The Enlightened Eye*. He draws from his life as an artist and teacher to challenge readers to think about new ways of seeing and solving problems in education. Eisner believes that seeing is central to one's effectiveness as a teacher and a researcher of classroom practices. Seeing, however, is more than looking at a classroom situation, a group, or an individual student. It requires an enlightened eye—the perception, meaning, and value of qualities, "that pervade intimate social relations and those that constitute complex social situations such as schools" (p. 1).

Insightful teachers have the ability to see or perceive what counts during classroom lessons and interactions with students. For example, insightful teachers have a sense of what is significant to focus on during an interaction or event; they have the ability to quickly sift out the unimportant features from critical ones. And they have the ability to understand the significance of what they see. As Philip Jackson noted in his book *The Practice of Teaching* (1986), expert teachers "see more...they are alive to the latent pedagogical possibilities in the events they witness...they anticipate what is going to happen...[and] their senses are fully tuned to what is going on around them" (p. 87). To develop the skills of perception, a teacher must practice "seeing" what he or she wants to understand (for example, individual students' learning, one's teaching, the conditions set up in a classroom that support learning, or the use of particular materials with a group of students). "Learning to see more" occurs when teachers engage in inquiry in which they describe, interpret, and evaluate actions and events, reflect on what they learn, and then act on this knowledge.

Generating Insights: An Example

As we learn more about developing insight, let's examine and describe the actions of Mr. Isobe in the story *Crow Boy* and think about the insights this teacher gleaned about a learner. First, this teacher *developed a relationship* with Chibi and, as a result, learned about the child as an individual. To accomplish this goal he spent time talking one-on-one with Chibi, learning about his family and interests. We can assume that he also observed Chibi during classroom lessons, including his *interactions with peers and teachers*, and studied previous records. This allowed the teacher to construct a portrait of Chibi as a learner. Mr. Isobe determined what Chibi knew, including Chibi's in-school and out-of-school knowledge. For example, Chibi knew a lot about plants and gardening from his family experiences. Chibi also knew a lot about literacy, representing his ideas in multiple ways (writing and drawing). Mr. Isobe recognized and highlighted what Chibi could do, as opposed to focusing on what he could not do.

Mr. Isobe also *set up conditions that supported Chibi's learning*. He respected the child's knowledge and perseverance and he expected other students to show respect for Chibi. He also developed a curriculum that built on Chibi's interests as well as the interests of the other students, and that ensured that Chibi could succeed at various tasks and activities within the curriculum. Finally, the teacher helped Chibi prepare for his performance of "Crow Voices," and in so doing, valued Chibi's knowledge and *supported his alternate form of representing his knowledge*—the arts.

Mr. Isobe gleaned many insights about Chibi and used this knowledge to shape learning experiences. He was insightful because he understood how others viewed Chibi's physical appearance and his seeming lack of intelligence. He also understood how Chibi's past history as a learner and his interactions, or lack thereof with peers and teachers, affected him as a learner and person. Isobe saw "the inner nature of things" viewing Chibi as a person, complete with hidden talents that were developed and honored outside school settings. Mr. Isobe used his insights to shape positive learning situations and to engage in supportive, informed pedagogy. He knew how to support Chibi's learning, understood what Chibi knew, valued this knowledge, helped Chibi build on his talents to achieve greater learning, and allowed Chibi to show others what he knew through alternate forms of representing knowledge. Mr. Isobe's insights about individual learners, relationships between teachers and students and between peers, conditions that support learning, and interactions between classroom participants allowed him to develop into a responsive, planful teacher. In the remainder of this book we will explore many of these key insights in more depth and further define the concept of culturally responsive and planful teaching.

Reflection Point

Describe an insightful teacher from your past. Which of this individual's characteristics stand out for you? How did his or her actions affect you as a learner?

Describe a moment of insight you've experienced about a learner.

Organization of the Rest of This Book

Developing insight to meet the needs of all children requires a new way of conceptualizing the processes of learning, teaching, and schooling. Many of you already have started to explore these ideas; I hope that you resonate with the ideas discussed here. In the remaining chapters I will present the following topics:

- Chapter 2: Insight requires a sense of where we are headed and how to get there. Where we are headed is our "end in view," or what we want teaching and learning to look like in our classroom practice. I will discuss moral purpose and vision; the role of inquiry, reflection, and writing in achieving our moral purpose and vision; and the characteristics of responsive, planful teachers.

- Chapter 3: Insight requires an understanding of where we have come from and recognition of our students' backgrounds. It is important to write about and reflect on our literacy histories as a way to understand our cultural backgrounds, past experiences, and the individuals who helped to shape our current beliefs about literacy teaching and learning. Likewise, it is important to understand the cultural backgrounds and literacy histories of our students, the knowledges they bring to school from home, and how we can build on this knowledge as we seek to meet students' literacy needs.

- Chapter 4: Insight requires identifying our beliefs and current practices, uncovering tensions between the two, and solving problems that arise daily in our classrooms. I will talk about several tensions identified by teachers and how they grappled with these issues. This discussion will position problems as "our friends" and seek innovative ways to solve them. A critical perspective of literacy will be introduced as one way to identify tensions.

- Chapter 5: Insight requires reconsidering the conditions of learning and relationships we build with students. Key to this goal is thinking about the current literature in the area of motivation and engagement and gleaning information about students' in-school and out-of-school literacy practices, their interests, and who they are as people. I also will discuss current research on teaching and learning.

- Chapter 6: Insight requires a close examination of literacy events and practices in our classrooms so we can focus on the relationships and interactions between peers and between teachers and students to understand how these conditions shape literacy learning for individual learners. In addition, new definitions of literacy emerge from closely observing children and their learning in and out of school.

- Chapter 7: Insight requires action. This final chapter presents ways to think about putting together the ideas presented in all chapters of the book into a coherent, useable plan.

Although the ideas in each chapter and across chapters are present-ed in a particular order, this is not intended to indicate steps that one might go through as they read and respond to ideas in the text. Instead, you may want to consider many of these ideas in a concurrent and spi-raling fashion. New ideas are layered on top of previously presented ideas and an attempt is made to connect ideas. It also should be noted that I am not presenting answers or *the* correct model of insightful teaching. Rather, I offer strategies for examining who we are, who our students are, and what we do as teachers and learners in classrooms that shapes learning in positive ways.

Chapter 2

Determining Where We Are Headed and How to Get There

I really care about these kids—I'm concerned about getting to know them—showing them that I want them to learn and do certain things but also that I care about who they are. I try to communicate that verbally, nonverbally, whatever. I teach kids—because they're all unique in a way and I like that. I can't remember anyone [student] that I disliked—that didn't have something redeeming about them. I want to be a teacher who makes a difference to kids, particularly the basic track kids. With some of these kids what you're teaching them with literature is not—I mean they are not going to remember who wrote The Pearl *or* Of Mice and Men, *and they may not even remember Lenny and George after 2 or 3 years. But they did something—they got involved in a book and they got involved in something where they used their imaginations. They had a good experience—they experienced something together which was good. They opened up and shared some of their thoughts and feelings which they may not ever do because they may be in a family situation where they get slapped for it or put down for it as they frequently are. And some of them go through our program [high school] only having two or three good experiences.*

Rick Umpleby

Michael Fullan's book, *Change Forces: Probing the Depths of Educational Reform* (1993), challenges educators to step back and consider the moral purpose in our professional lives and create a personal vision by posing a fundamental question: What difference am I trying to make? As we examine Rick's vision that begins this chapter it is clear that he has a moral purpose that undergirds his actions. He is passionate about the students he teaches and his role as an educator, and he is dedicated to making a difference in their lives. He feels that all students—regardless of their ability level or background—deserve the opportunity to learn, to be excited about their learning, and to be successful at school tasks. Rick also values the idea that students need to develop skills, and he views this as an equally important teaching mission. He believes there are ways to help students develop the knowledge, skills, and dispositions they need by getting them involved in learning processes and ensuring that they have positive experiences in school.

Another key characteristic of Rick Umpleby is his desire to constantly seek ways to improve his pedagogy. He is hoping to meet even the most difficult teaching challenge and support the students who most need his guidance. He also collaborates with colleagues who want to make a difference in the lives of learners. In his own unique way, he is a change agent.

Where Are We Headed? A Moral Purpose to Direct Our Actions

Fullan (1993) notes that to meet the needs of learners in the 21st century, educators must become effective change agents who have a *moral purpose* to their professional endeavors. John Goodlad, Roger Soder, and Kenneth Sirotnik (1990), well-known in the area of educational renewal, wrote a book titled *The Moral Dimensions of Teaching* in which they discuss the fact that moral purposes are "fundamental normative positions derived from moral and ethical arguments that serve to ground appropriate answers to crucial educational questions" (p. xi). For example, the authors note that moral purposes are constructed based on answers to questions such as, Whose interests are served and whose should be served in our schools? What is the relationship of the interests of the individual, family, community, and society?

Fullan (1993) identifies an important moral purpose that fits perfectly with the goals of the Kids InSight series: "to make a difference in the lives of students regardless of background, and to help produce citizens who can live and work productively in increasingly dynamically complex societies" (p. 4). I believe this is the ultimate goal of many educators—it is the reason we dedicate our lives to learners and the field of teaching. Likewise, John Dewey, noted educational philosopher, states that teachers should have a moral aim of creating "a freer and more humane experience" for all (cited in Boisvert, 1998, p. 299), contributing to the ultimate goal of democracy. And Rorty (1982), a pragmatist, reminds us that "what matters is our loyalty to other human beings, clinging together against the dark, not our hopes of getting things right" (p. 166).

Effective teachers who are continually working to remake good schools into better ones are in the process of *renewal*, and they work according to a plan. A plan allows a moral purpose to be met efficiently and well. For example, Goodlad et al. (1990) created a plan or an agenda for renewal called the Agenda for Education in a Democracy. Gary Fenstermacher (1999), in *Leadership for Educational Renewal* (Smith & Fenstermacher, 1999), reviews the four basic principles or moral dimensions that form the foundation for the agenda for what schools, teaching, and learning should be about. This plan includes two opening statements that focus on worthy ends for schooling; the third and fourth statements identify important teaching practices that allow us to attain the first two moral dimensions:

- To facilitate the critical enculturation of the young into a social and political democracy.
- To provide all children and youths disciplined encounters with all subject matters of the human conversation.
- To engage in pedagogical practices that forge a caring and effective connection between teacher and student.
- To exercise responsible stewardship of our schools. (p. 11)

The first dimension, enculturating the young into a democracy, goes beyond the idea of preparing young people with particular skills or understandings about democracy. It also includes helping students develop traits such as "tolerance, fairness, caring, openness, critical judgement, and a due regard for evidence" (p. 13).

The second dimension, providing disciplined encounters with all subject matters, is based on the idea that all students, regardless of cultural or academic background, should be allowed fair and equal access to knowledge and the opportunity to understand concepts. This statement would cause the practice of tracking to be questioned because it often limits low-achieving students from encountering quality materials. It also calls into question the idea that only the highest achieving students can learn to think critically while lower achieving students must focus on skills work before they tackle critical ideas or ways of thinking.

The third dimension, engaging in a nurturant pedagogy, focuses on the idea that teachers must not only engage students in subject matter in ways in which they understand important concepts and learn to think in critical ways, but we need to connect learning with students' life experiences. Adhering to this dimension also means that as teachers seek to help develop students' cognitively and affectively, we also work to engage students as fellow human beings. Thus, the focus is not only on what students learn and how they learn, but on the quality of relationships between teachers and students—relationships that influence all learning.

Teaching is complex, and many problems arise on a daily basis. It is easy for individuals to blame problems on "the system." Teachers who exercise responsible stewardship, Fenstermacher's fourth dimension, see that they are part of the system, and as such must contribute to the good of the whole as well as to themselves or the colleagues they work with most closely. It is worth remembering that we benefit from membership in communities or systems—we depend on them for support and for a sense of belonging. But membership and a sense of belonging require some self-sacrifice in terms of fulfilling promises, keeping confidences, and foregoing constant self-interest for the good of others.

Fenstermacher goes on to explain that these statements are the moral dimensions on which teachers build visions, missions, and agendas for renewing their practice. Thus, a key message in the research presented here is that identifying one's moral purpose, reflecting on it, and using it to affect our actions is critical to effective teaching and learning. It is important for us to do this as literacy educators. Pause for a few moments here and write responses to the following Reflection Point questions in your journal.

*Reflection Point*_____

What is your moral purpose as an educator? As a literacy educator? How is your moral purpose indicated through your practices?

_____

There is no one "politically correct" moral purpose. Rather, there are ways to test the soundness of your ideas. Look back at the moral dimensions presented in this section. How do your ideas about moral purpose fit within these broad guidelines? What would people from outside your classroom see that shows your moral purpose in action as they watch you and your students during lessons?

A Moral Purpose in Practice: The Role of Caring

Joe Ruhl, the high school biology teacher introduced in Chapter 1, made the following remarks about his students and the role of caring for them that influences his pedagogy in an interview session with me.

> I care about my students—I want them to feel special—to relate to them as persons. I do this in part by sharing my own experiences with learners. I strive to stimulate the kids' sense of wonder and curiosity with learning activities that are interesting and relevant. Along with biology I hope to teach them the importance of self-discipline, time management, and meeting strict deadlines. Finally, I try to help my kids build self-confidence in their own abilities as students—to help them discover that goal setting and hard work will, in the end, lead to success.

In the vignette that opens this chapter and the one immediately above, we see the concept of caring about learners identified as a moral dimension needed to ground our teaching, and expressed by both Rick Umpleby and Joe Ruhl as central to their teaching goals. *Caring* is a key component of a teacher's moral purpose and can be expressed in the formal and informal interactions between teachers and students, in the classroom contexts constructed by teachers and students, and in the materials selected and activities designed for and used by students.

In an issue of *Phi Delta Kappan* devoted exclusively to the issue of caring, Chaskin and Rauner (1995) define caring as

> the ways in which individuals and institutions protect young people and invest in their ongoing development. It also involves the ways in which young people, in turn, protect the rights and interests of others and ultimately support the ongoing development of their social and civic communities. (pp. 671–672)

Caring in practice is grounded in relationships and action and is based on the needs that all individuals have for "interdependence and connection, for belonging and membership, for safety and support, and for individual and social competency" (p. 672).

In relating the concept of caring to a teacher's moral purpose, I am reminded of the book *The Cathedral Within: Transforming Your Life by Giving Something Back* by Bill Shore (1999). In this book the author discusses how individuals give something back to others (society) through public service. He notes that the "cathedral within each of us" is the spiritual aspect to our work. By giving of ourselves to others, we transform our lives. However, like a cathedral building, an individual's work with others is never complete, nor are our efforts necessarily visible in our lifetime. And, charitable intentions alone do not result in positive outcomes for others. Rather, by acting in an informed manner and collaborating with others to create a community of wealth, we can make good things happen.

BOX 2-1
Resources on the Topic of Caring

Eaker-Rich, D., & Van Galen, J. (1996). *Caring in an unjust world: Negotiating borders and barriers in schools*. New York: State University of New York Press.

Noddings, N. (1986). *Caring: A feminine approach to ethics and moral education*. Berkeley, CA: University of California Press.

Noddings, N. (1992). *The challenge to care in schools: An alternative approach to education*. New York: Teachers College Press.

Shore's "cathedral within" analogy certainly fits the teaching profession and the concept of moral purpose. As we know, often we do not see the results of our efforts with learners until years later when former students visit our classrooms or send a letter reminding us that our time spent listening to a problem or helping them understand a concept made a lasting impression on them. Caring about students as learners and people is very much a moral purpose that impacts teaching and learning. This is a theme that will thread throughout the remainder of this book. (See Box 2-1 for resources on the topic of caring.)

Achieving One's Moral Purpose: The Role of Change

The needs of learners make it imperative that *all* educators seek a moral purpose and the habits and skills that accompany it. It is important to remember that moral purposes are not just ideas that come from within us. Our ideas must be shaped by outside forces—particularly the needs and interests of the students we teach. As Fullan (1993) notes, making a difference for learners must be "recast in broader social and moral terms" (p. 11), and the broader contexts or dimensions that surround teaching must be addressed. This implies that changing teaching and learning practices must occur at the institutional level or with teams of educators while occurring simultaneously at the individual level. Individual change agents who engage in change processes understand that this process is complex and nonlinear and is full of risk-taking, frustration, and failure. But teachers recognize that the positive outcomes of their change processes outweigh the fears and concerns. For change agents the process ultimately is exciting and rewarding, and is the only hope we have for truly making a difference for learners and improving our own professional lives. Sometimes we think that we cannot change our practices because we believe that institutional complexities are too great to surmount. But each of us has a great deal of control over our own motives and skills as educators. This begs the question, How does one become a change agent?

In *Change Forces* (1993), Fullan discusses several key components for educators to consider as they work to renew their practices and make substantive changes in students' learning schoolwide and in individual class-rooms. These components include the following:

1. Teachers are urged to recommit themselves to a moral purpose as educators. This purpose must be at the forefront of all efforts.

2. Teachers benefit from creating personal vision statements, ground-ed in their moral purpose and solidified by current, sound knowl-edge about teaching and learning, subject area knowledge, curriculum, pedagogy, and policy issues.

3. Educators are urged to recognize the links between the moral pur-poses that ground their work at the school level and larger issues of educational policy and societal development.

4. While developing their own personal visions, teachers will find it useful to also work collaboratively with other educators and individ-uals outside school settings to create shared visions and purposes.

5. To create new visions and plans to carry out these visions, new structures for working together will be required of collaborative teams.

6. To facilitate the processes outlined in the five points above, teachers are urged to develop the habits and skills of continuous inquiry and learning, seeking new ideas from inside and outside school sources.

7. Teachers need to be aware of, and commit to, the positive and neg-ative components of educational change—the highs of small suc-cesses and the lows of things getting worse before they get better. It means that we must acknowledge the tensions and confusion in-herent in change processes and the idea that vision and planning do not always precede action (sometimes we do not see possibilities as they unfold over time). However, vision and planning cannot be left out of our ongoing renewal efforts.

The seven components listed here are not a step-by-step process to be followed, although some appear to build on the others. For example, the creation of a vision does not precede inquiry into one's teaching, al-though thinking about one's vision certainly helps this process. Rather, vision may be advanced, reshaped, and questioned through the process of inquiry into teaching and learning. Renewing one's practices and making substantive changes in students' learning is a continuous, recursive process. What is critical when addressing these seven points is a desire to improve one's practice, characterized by the notion that improvement is possible; the willingness to be self-critical; the ability to recognize better practices than one's own; and the willingness to learn what must be learned to move forward (Nias, Southworth, & Campbell, 1992). Key to this process is the belief in, and adherence to, a moral purpose and vision that sets this purpose in motion and serves as a touchstone for all other actions.

Linking Moral Purpose and Vision

Joe Ruhl had a vision for his academic-track biology class at Lafayette High School, as noted in these remarks:

> After years of seeing students turned off to science lectures and taking tests that indicated that many concepts still remained a mystery, I decided to revamp my teaching philosophy and approach. I rejected the idea of a bell curve in learning and embraced the idea of mastery learning. I don't want students to just sit in my classes and listen to lectures. Instead, I want them to actively work together in study groups, "struggling"—talking and reading about ideas and collaboratively crafting responses—to complete guides designed to support the learning of important concepts. I also want them to participate in labs designed to enhance particular concepts and make science class more interesting. At the end of a unit, students will take Form A of a unit test and if they don't pass this with 80% or higher mastery, then they can complete practice activities covering the concepts they didn't understand before taking Form B of the unit test. I just don't feel it is productive to keep moving through more content when kids don't understand the concepts we've just investigated. I would rather not cover so much content during the semester to ensure that the kids learn the ideas we do focus on. Overall my vision is for all students—those who want to pursue science careers and those who don't—to become scientifically literate by participating in biology class, and as a result become contributing members of society. I believe that the way to attain my vision is to treat all students as people able to learn, and I will strive to make learning meaningful and fun.

As noted in Fullan's second point outlined earlier, the linking of a personal vision with a moral purpose is crucial. A *vision* is taking our ideal—

to make a difference in the lives of learners—and making it explicit and "doable"—in this case stating *what* we want to accomplish and *how* we plan to make a difference in the lives of learners. Vision-building requires that we ask ourselves important questions regarding our beliefs about teaching and learning that heretofore may have remained implicit and unarticulated. And crafting our vision requires that we take a proactive, positive stand on issues that we value—that we reach for high goals, stating publicly what we believe. It would be easy to fall back on excuses that many of us have used, such as "I can't teach the way I'd like to because I don't have the resources or time to plan and enact my ideas" or "My colleagues and administrators are not supportive of my efforts." Instead, we must push ourselves to reconsider and connect our teaching efforts to the betterment of society, working against the status quo and toward purposeful change that might effect deeper change at the organizational (school and district) level.

Many people caution that visions created at the beginning of the change process blind people or constrain future actions. This is why I refer to the need to *begin* to build a vision to provide a thoughtful starting point. However, it is critical to realize that our personal vision statements should not remain static, nor should they change with the latest trend in education. Rather, one's vision serves as a way to test new ideas, theories, and proposed curricula. The initial draft statement is a work-in-progress that continually begs for revision and fine-tuning. For example, Joe Ruhl's initial vision statement created prior to the school year was revised several times over the year based on his analysis of students' papers, his formal and informal interactions with students, and the insights he gleaned from listening to and observing students as they worked in groups on activities.

Visions are often crafted by educators based on dissatisfaction with, or questions pertaining to, one's current practices. An example of this dissatisfaction with traditional ways of teaching and learning are evident in Joe's vision. He was concerned that content coverage was becoming more important than student learning, he was worried that he had not designed learning activities that students connected with and that helped them glean important concepts, and he was troubled by the fact that all students did not view science as important to their lives. Joe was committed to uncovering the tensions and challenges that occurred on a daily basis and to critically examining how events were enacted. He also was constantly asking himself why learning was successful for some students, but others did not experience the same level of success. Later in this chapter, we will explore a revision Joe made to his vision based on analyzing data from his classroom.

From my observations, crafting vision statements and enacting them is one hallmark of an effective teacher. Effective teachers have moral purpose, informed belief systems, and a vision that is constantly being updated and refined. They have skills and the ability of how to put knowledge and skills into practice. They are committed to students; they are caring, motivated, insightful, and reflective; and they are able to make discretionary judgments on the spot. Last, these teachers are not afraid to ask difficult questions of themselves and of others. They are constantly seeking to improve their practice through personal inquiry and work with others. I invite readers to pause a moment and write responses to the following questions to facilitate reflection, then analyze your responses before moving on to the next section of the chapter.

Reflection Point

What is your personal literacy teaching vision? What type of support structures exist in your school and district to assist you as you work to carry out your vision?

How Do We Achieve Our Moral Purpose and Vision? The Role of Inquiry, Reflection, and Writing

Researchers have found that educators with a nonexistent or limited sense of moral purpose and vision are never called on to demonstrate their commitment to learners and the field of education. Further, some visionary teachers never realize their abilities, and some are even thwarted. But, as Fullan (1993) notes, moral purpose and vision are not enough. Teachers also must have the knowledge base and pedagogical skills needed to work with a variety of learners, and have the habits and skills required to "engage in continuous corrective analysis and action" (p. 5). Sarason (1990) notes that educators should have the same goal for themselves as they set for students—to develop into lifelong learners:

> Should not our aim be to judge whatever we do for our children in our schools by the criterion of how we are fostering the desire to continue to learn about self, others, and the world, to live in the world of ideas and possibilities, to see the life span as an endless intellectual and personal quest for knowledge and meaning? (p. 163)

The Role of Inquiry

Inquiry involves looking closely at classroom practices and asking questions pertaining to teaching, learners and learning, activities, structures, texts, tasks, and interactions, always asking what dialogue, events, and actions seem to mean and seeking more than surface-level answers. This process of asking questions helps educators frame an issue or problem they want to investigate. When a question or problem is defined, the individual or event to be studied is identified. Sometimes this question changes as we engage in inquiry, or the question is shaped by what is learned. To find answers to certain issues, educators select appropriate sources from which to collect data. Teacher-researchers survey and observe learners, interview and collect artifacts such as students' work, and typically draw from multiple data sources to gather information. These data are analyzed using a variety of tools and strategies, and are interpreted to generate patterns or possible explanations. The inquiry process also may involve standardized tests and formal instruments, and data may be reduced to numbers or scores. Ways of engaging in inquiry are based in large part on a teacher's purpose for the research and how the findings will be used.

Second, inquiry is the desire to read current and historical research articles that are published in journals, monographs, books, and technical reports to learn about what works in particular settings for certain teachers and students. Often this research includes descriptions of teacher-researcher inquiry, in which an educator documents his or her work in classrooms, identifies teaching dilemmas, and outlines the processes teachers engage in as they work to meet the needs of all learners. (See Box 2-2 for resources on how to engage in teacher inquiry, and see Box 2-3 for examples of teacher inquiry studies.)

BOX 2-2
Books That Address Teacher Inquiry

Eisenhart, M.A., & Borko, H. (1993). *Designing classroom research: Themes, issues, and struggles.* Boston: Allyn & Bacon.

Glesne, C., & Peshkin, A. (1992). *Becoming qualitative researchers: An introduction.* White Plains, NY: Longman.

Hitchcock, G., & Hughes, D. (1992). *Research and the teacher: A qualitative introduction to school-based research.* New York: Routledge.

Hubbard, R.S., & Power, B.M. (1999). *Living the questions: A guide for teacher-researchers.* York, ME: Stenhouse.

Olson, M.W. (1990). *Opening the door to classroom research.* Newark, DE: International Reading Association.

Pinnell, G.S., & Matlin, M.L. (1989). *Teachers and research: Language learning in the classroom.* Newark, DE: International Reading Association.

BOX 2-3
Teacher Inquiry Studies

Avery, C. (1993). *...And with a light touch: Learning about reading, writing, and teaching with first graders.* Portsmouth, NH: Heinemann.

Bissex, G.L., & Bullock, R.H. (1987). *Seeing for ourselves: Case study research by teachers of writing.* Portsmouth, NH: Heinemann.

Fraser, J., & Skolnick, D. (1994). *On their way: Celebrating second graders as they read and write.* Portsmouth, NH: Heinemann.

Paley, V.G. (1979). *White teacher.* Cambridge MA: Harvard University Press.

Paley, V.G. (1990). *The boy who would be a helicopter.* Cambridge, MA: Harvard University Press.

Rose, M. (1989). *Lives on the boundary: The struggles and achievements of America's underprepared.* New York: Penguin

Rose, M. (1995). *Possible lives: The promise of public education in America.* New York: Houghton Mifflin.

Schmidt, P.A. (1997). *Beginning in retrospect: Writing and reading a teacher's life.* New York: Teachers College Press.

Third, inquiry involves collecting data and artifacts from students for use in learning about their development and processes and how these shape the pedagogies in which we engage. For example, it is useful to collect running records of young learners' oral reading of stories to see how these children use strategies to process texts and make sense of what they read, and to compile samples of students' writing across a semester to provide evidence for topics explored and growth in the ability to communicate messages. Teacher observation notes, interviews with students, and reflective writings about students' affective development also are important data sources. Most teachers engage in cross data analysis to construct a profile of a student's learning processes and products. (See Box 2-4 for texts to use in data collection.)

These multiple forms of inquiry provide an internal (personal) and external (others and classroom settings) view required to address the complexity of teaching and learning. Questions that teachers might ask include the following:

- To what extent do I engage in inquiry into what I do and how to do it better?

- To what extent do I consume, critique, and produce knowledge?

BOX 2-4
Texts to Use to Collect Data From Students

Barrentine, S.J. (Ed.). (1999). *Reading assessment: Principles and practices for elementary teachers.* Newark, DE: International Reading Association.

Farr, R.C., & Tone, B. (1998). *Portfolio and performance assessment: Helping students evaluate their progress as readers and writers* (2nd ed.). New York: Harcourt Brace.

Harp, B. (1996). *Handbook of literacy assessment and evaluation.* Norwood, MA: Christopher-Gordon.

Johnston, P.H. (1992). *Constructive evaluation of literate activity.* White Plains, NY: Longman.

Johnston, P.H. (1997). *Knowing literacy: Constructive literacy assessment.* York, ME: Stenhouse.

Rhodes, L.K. (1993). *Literacy assessment: A handbook of instruments.* Portsmouth, NH: Heinemann.

Rhodes, L.K., & Shanklin, N. (1993). *Windows into literacy: Assessing learners K–8.* Portsmouth, NH: Heinemann.

Strickland, K., & Strickland, J. (2000). *Making assessment elementary.* Portsmouth, NH: Heinemann.

- To what extent do I engage competently in discourse (talk about my thoughts, actions, and reflections) and take action to improve my teaching and students' learning?
- To what extent do I focus on my needs and interests when engaging in inquiry versus those of other educators and my students?

The Role of Reflection

Reflection—stopping to write, think about, question, and test one's assumptions, actions, and experiences—is key to effective teaching but it is not an activity that "just happens." Instead, reflection is a learned practice that is most effective when practiced over time. For example, in *Beginning in Retrospect: Writing and Reading a Teacher's Life* (1997), English teacher Patricia Schmidt writes about the importance of keeping the papers she wrote so she could reflect on them to understand the teacher she was becoming. Reflective teachers develop the ability to describe their actions or interactions or to write about teaching experiences or dilemmas. These teachers then reflect on or analyze the resulting description or narrative. Reflective teachers are also *reflexive*—that is, they are able to "turn in" on themselves to question assumptions about knowledge. This concept takes the reflective process one step further to one of uncovering and critiquing that which may not be observable.

Schmidt's book is an example of how the reflection process allowed one teacher to engage in self-exploration that she hoped might result in change. As Schmidt notes, "Change meant that I had to face my fears, name them, and begin to take risks in spite of them" (p. 87). Schmidt recommends two publications for teachers to read who wish to explore their personal and teaching lives: *Psychology for Teachers: An Alternative Approach* (1988) by Philla Salmon and *When Teachers Face Themselves* (1955) by Arthur Jersild.

In *The Reflective Practitioner: How Professionals Think in Action* (1987), Donald Schon, a leader in the area of reflective teaching, discusses how experienced teachers execute teaching and learning activities without having to think about them. He refers to this phenomenon as "knowing-in-action" (pp. 26–31). On occasion, however, a familiar routine results in an unexpected outcome. These are either unpleasant or pleasant surprises that teachers dismiss or reflect on in one of two ways: The first of these is "to reflect on action" (look back) to determine how our knowing-in-action may have shaped the surprise event. This sometimes happens after or during an event, resulting in the reshaping of our actions in progress called "reflect-in-action." Reflection causes us to critically question our knowing-in-action and we may develop new strategies, understandings, or ways of thinking. Second, we may chose to experiment on the spot as we test the new knowledge we have gleaned to change things for the better. The end result is that our future actions are influenced by what we learn.

In his article, "Zen and the Art of Reflective Practice in Teacher Education," Robert Tremmel (1993) writes about reflection and asserts that as teachers we must become self-aware as we teach and engage in critical self-reflection. Being mentally aware, Tremmel notes, means that we learn to pay attention to what is occurring in our classrooms as well as understanding who we are and how this shapes our actions. Paying attention is facilitated when we become more mindful of students, when we become aware of our own thoughts and feelings as we teach and afterward, and when we write and talk with others about our experiences and dilemmas. As Tremmel notes, "Looking within is part of preparing ourselves for—and actually engaging in—reflective and mindful practice" (p. 455). (See Box 2-5 for additional resources on the reflective process.)

From Schon and Tremmel's work we learn that insight about learners and our pedagogy necessitates that educators develop the ability to re-

---

BOX 2-5
Resources on the Reflective Process

Clift, R.T., Houston, R.W., & Pugach, M.C. (Eds.). (1990). *Encouraging reflective practice in education: An analysis of issues and programs.* New York: Teachers College Press.

Schon, D.A. (Ed.) (1991). *The reflective turn: Case studies in and on educational practice.* New York: Teachers College Press.

Tremmel, R. (1993). Zen and the art of reflective practice in teacher education. *Harvard Education Review, 63*(4), 434–458.

Witherell, C., & Noddings, N. (Eds.). (1991). *Stories lives tell: Narrative and dialogue in education.* New York: Teachers College Press.

flect-in-action and then produce a good verbal or written description of what happened and reflect on this product. Schon notes that this reflection-in-action "begins a dialogue of thinking and doing through which [one] becomes more skillful" (p. 31). This is a goal for teachers interested in becoming more insightful and learning to keep their students in sight.

The Role of Writing

In thinking about the power of writing as a tool for learning, many of us defer to the research conducted by Flower and Hayes (1981, 1984) in which they talk about the idea that writing reflects thinking, and is, in fact, a form of thinking. Likewise, Harry Wolcott, a noted educational anthropologist, has written about the power of writing when researchers are trying to make sense of their observations or emerging theories. He notes that writing helps us discover gaps in our thinking or when we "seem not to be thinking at all" (1990, p. 21).

Teachers who engage in inquiry and seek to be reflective in the process are able to glean insights about themselves and students as they write. Writing is an activity that becomes part of reflective practitioners' daily ritual, as opposed to a culminating activity at the end of a teaching unit, semester, or inquiry project. As noted previously, writing helps teachers record events and ideas and analyze issues, it provides a forum to explore interpretations about events to sharpen our focus as we engage in future inquiry activities, and it allows us to share with ourselves and others what we have learned. As Carol Witherell and Nell Noddings (1991) comment in their book, *Stories Lives Tell: Narrative and Dialogue in Education*, telling, writing, reading, and listening to life stories creates a powerful opportunity to learn. Teachers can "penetrate cultural barriers, discover the power of self and the integrity of the other, and deepen their understanding of their respective histories and possibilities" (p. 4).

Linking Inquiry, Reflection, and Writing

The following story, written by teacher-researcher Vivian Paley (1997), illustrates how inquiry, reflection, and writing are interrelated and key to understanding what our students know and can teach us about learning processes and what we can learn about ourselves:

> I tried to avoid paths of inquiry in which it would necessarily be my own behavior that would be examined and found wanting. The idiosyncratic thoughts that both astonished and disheartened me concerned the possibility that I did not view every child in the same favorable light. Having made the awful discovery that my expectations for Black children might be lower than those I held for White children, my fate was sealed. I would forever be searching for the truth behind all this and all other carefully hidden cover-ups that surrounded me in the classroom. (p. vii)

Paley talks about the power of studying events in classrooms closely and pondering their meaning. She notes that as teachers study their actions, talking about what they learn is not enough to foster self-examination and reflection. Rather, she believes that significant alterations in our actions occur when we write about our teaching because there "is no other way to listen to ourselves think" (p. viii).

James Pennebaker (1997) also advocates the power of writing to change lives in his book *Opening Up: The Healing Power of Expressing Emotions*. In writing about people who have used writing after experiencing a trauma in their lives, the author found that writing in a journal a small amount of time each day (10–20 minutes) resulted positively for these individuals. Further, individuals who wrote and talked about issues had increased brain energy and ability to solve problems as compared to individuals who merely thought about or mulled over issues.

In sum, insightful teachers observe, collect data samples, and talk with students to understand classroom events and children's ideas and perspectives on these events. These teachers write about what they have observed and learned and through this process learn to reflect and think about their practices. Teachers also seek insights from research journals and conferences, particularly when students' needs are identified through careful observation. Finally, insightful teachers are not afraid to reconsider their practices. They do not change for the sake of change but have thoughtful reasons for their actions that are usually grounded in research and what works in classrooms to promote students' learning.

In the Kids InSight series, multiple opportunities are provided for readers to inquire and write as a strategy for addressing issues we are worried about or wish to understand better in our classrooms. However, as Paley (1997) notes, even though inquiry, writing, and reflection are important to our future practices, these practices alone will not result in definitive answers. Why? Students come to us with new ideas and new ways of learning, and thus, we must expect to continually generate new explanations about our teaching and students' learning. We will revisit the concepts of inquiry and reflection throughout this book.

Observing Inquiry, Reflection, and Writing in Action

The following section is an example of inquiry, reflection, and writing based on a collaborative research project in Joe Ruhl's biology classroom. I present a segment from an analysis session my colleague David O'Brien and I had with Joe one evening after school. We were reading a transcript of one small-group session in which the students were working on a portion of a study guide. The audiotape of the groupwork session and the transcript generated from it were data sources we were using in our research project in which we were studying the teaching and learning processes in Joe's classroom. Specifically, Joe wanted to know what and how students were learning during groupwork and their perspectives on the value of study guides. As we analyzed a transcript from a class discussion, a teaching dilemma arose for Joe.

Carolyn, Joey, Jay, and Brian worked together in a self-selected cooperative learning group answering questions on their high school biology study guide. At this point in the lesson, the students were using their textbook and study guide to answer questions designed to help them understand the life cycle of the sheep liver fluke and the tapeworm. The instruction on the study guide read, "You have already looked at the life cycle of the sheep liver fluke on page 390. Now draw a life cycle diagram for the tapeworm below. Include the larva (in a cyst), and human."

Carolyn:	Did you read that one thing [the guide] for the, uh, question?
Joey:	No.

Brian: It's supposed to be from there...(pointing to a section in the textbook) to there—it should tell [about the life cycle of the tapeworm].

Joey: It *should* tell. (Carolyn repeats "should!")

Brian: Should! Mr. Ruhl said it would.

Carolyn: Why couldn't they [the textbook book publishers/authors] just have diagrams [of the tapeworm cycle] or something?

(a few moments later)

Joey: Here's where it says [about the tapeworm]—the last paragraph (pointing to a portion of the book).

Carolyn: The last paragraph (she points in the textbook).

Jay: It doesn't really say how, how the...

Carolyn: (reading from the textbook) It may involve one, two, or three different... (inaudible—a few students are reading at the same time) it's transmitted by infected pork, beef, or, well...

Joey: I haven't had this much fun in...

Jay: A cow produces the, the tape grows up in the cow then, then the cow gets rid of it.

Joey: No, then the cow, it's in the cow's body, he gets rid of it...

Jay: The cow eats the grass.... It goes into, it goes...(Joey says "inside the cow") inside the cow and the human eats the cow, then the human gets it. That's how it works.

Carolyn: (not understanding) Yeah, but then how does the... (she's interrupted)

Brian: That's all we need, OK?

Carolyn: I think we need more than that.

Joey: When the human gets rid of its waste, the larva...

Carolyn: ...go back into the ground

Joey: ...produce. I'm sticking with this...

Carolyn: ...no, OK, it's, um...

Joey: I'm sticking with it.

Carolyn: I know but it goes out with, uh,

Jay: ...the waste.

Carolyn: It goes out with the waste, right?

Jay: Yes, I hope so.

Carolyn:	And so then, um, and then it's picked up by another, um, cow.
Brian:	Yeah.
Carolyn:	And then the cow, um, inside of the cow it...
Joey:	It grows.
Carolyn:	...it grows. And then it produces larva which is...
Jay:	Eggs and then it can...
Joey:	Yeah, that's how it works.

We stopped our reading of the transcript and listening to the audiotape at this point and Joe, David, and I talked about what was happening during groupwork. Joe noted that the students were struggling with the concepts on the guide and that he was pleased to see everyone contributing to the dialogue. He also began to see where they were having trouble making connections in the life cycle and he was pleased that Carolyn was not satisfied with an easy answer. As Joe noted, "I wish I could have stepped in here to help redirect the group's efforts but I was across the room at this point working with another group." We continued our analysis by reading more of the transcript of the group session and listening to the tape.

Carolyn:	If the pork isn't exactly [cooked well enough]. If it's, when it's transmitted, if the pork isn't exactly...
Jay:	Are we doing a cow or a pig?
Joey:	We're doing a cow—it says cow.
Carolyn:	Well if meat isn't thoroughly cooked...
Brian:	Well it just says infected animal, it could be a dog, OK?
Carolyn:	Would you eat a dog?
Brian:	It could be a dog.
Carolyn:	I'm not going to eat a dog.
Brian:	It says infected animal (laughing).
Carolyn:	Go eat a dog! Get a real life.
Joey:	I bet you've ate a horse before.
Brian:	No, I'm very picky on what I eat.

Carolyn:	I'm very picky in the meat section. (Jay laughs and says "yeah") And make sure it makes me big and strong. (Jay mentions "processed horse meat")
Brian:	They say *cow* on there [the study guide]. It actually could be processed horse meat.
Carolyn:	Processed horse (laughing). That's probably what they feed us here at school.
Jay:	You actually eat the school food?
Brian:	No.
Carolyn:	I try my hardest not to.
Brian:	I never eat it.

Joe stopped the tape at this point. "Yes, this is the point where I realized that this group needed to be reorganized—see, they are goofing off. They have no leader. I remember that they were laughing and were really behind the other groups at this point in time. That's why I decided to break them up and put each one in another group with a strong leader. I think this will work well." I then asked Joe, "But they seem to be having fun and they enjoy working together—will splitting them up be a detriment to their learning? And what about the struggling stuff? Are they still doing this even though it takes them a while to address issues on the study guide?" David responded, "Yeah, I was thinking about a group session I was part of the other night and we spent time socializing and the other time getting our task completed!" We all laughed realizing that the social and academic components of tasks are a real part of all groupwork. We continued reading and listening to the group as they returned to the task on the study guide.

| Jay: | I think it's different (He pulls the group back to the conversation before the school lunch digression). I think it's the cow, um, the cow eats the humans, no, no...(the rest all laugh) the cow, OK, that part's right. The larva gets into the cow by the cow eating the grass that has the larva on it. And then, and then we eat the cow. But then before that if the cow gets rid of its waste and then the, um, the larva jumps on other grass and then the other cows eat it, that's how it gets to other cows. |

Joey:	Well yeah, yeah, but this is... [the question is asking something different]
Jay:	But it has to be a cycle, I mean it ends right there.
Brian:	No.
Jay:	Yeah it does.
Joey:	No it doesn't.
Brian:	It can't keep going. Cause these guys [cows]...
Joey:	It gets rid of its waste.
Brian:	We [humans] get rid of it and it goes back into the ground.
Jay:	In a cow field [humans get rid of it in a cow field]? (They all laugh and talk at the same time.)
Carolyn:	No, because...Mr. Ruhl? Mr. Ruhl?!! (calling the teacher to help).
Ruhl:	Just a second, yeah.
Brian:	How do they [cows] transport that junk [tapeworm]?
Ruhl:	Do you guys need serious help?

David, Joe, and I had an interesting discussion after the analysis session ended. Here is an excerpt from Joe's researcher journal, where he reflected on what he learned from closely examining the actions of his students and talking with other researchers about what actions and interactions seemed to indicate about learning.

> My goal as a biology teacher is for all of my students to become scientifically literate, even those not planning a career in the field of science. The mastery learning system was designed to support all students' learning of biology concepts and I wanted students to work cooperatively in small groups, talking or struggling over concepts as they complete study guides. During the liver fluke lesson I was monitoring all groups, traveling around the room and assisting students who, after working together, still had difficulty with the material. The group outlined in the transcript called me over to help them at the end of the period. This group appeared to be behind the other groups and seemed to be floundering with no group leader. I helped them with the concept they were having difficulty with and made a mental note to mix-up the groups the next day, moving all members of this group to different groups with strong leaders.
>
> However, when I read the lesson transcript I realized that despite the socializing periods between the on-task groupwork, this bunch of kids were doing the struggling and thinking I promoted as a way to learn biology concepts. Unlike students in other groups who were intent on merely

getting through the study guide, these students felt the need to clarify for themselves and their group members the concepts they were to learn. I realized that what I saw on the surface (a bunch of talking and laughing and kids behind the other groups in completing the guide) as I attempted to monitor all groups and meet the needs of individual students, wasn't the complete picture of what students were learning, how they were learning, and why they needed certain conditions under which to learn. I now recognize that students have multiple agendas—social and academic. I need to work to adapt my agenda to theirs so that there is some sort of common ground where students are engaged in the process of learning and at the same time are able to feel safe and have fun as they learn.

This example from Joe's journal shows that hi s observations, discussions with other researchers, journal writing, and reflections allowed him to develop insights into his teaching and students' learning processes. But Joe's insight required time and distance to examine data and the ability to look below the surface-level features of interactions and events; it also required setting aside his preconceived ideas about what learning should look like. Joe was confronted with rethinking what is considered on-task behavior and learning. He recognized that the students could socialize and still complete their work, and that talking about work while socializing might just result in discourse that promotes learning. Joe came to value students' needs and agendas and he sought ways to build on and mesh these with his own goals for students' learning. From reflecting on what occurred during the lesson, Joe shifted his practices in ways that reflected what he had learned. New areas for inquiry also emerged and we collaboratively designed a student interview guide to learn more about how learners perceived groupwork and what activities they felt helped them learn in biology class.

The example from Joe's classroom supports the notion that the process of writing, reflecting, collecting and analyzing data, reading, reconsidering, and reconceptualizing is not linear. In fact, readers will engage in many of these activities simultaneously. As Fullan (1993) notes, change is a journey not a blueprint; it is nonlinear and loaded with uncertainty. For example, Fullan notes that educators should reconsider past organization research that promotes the idea that we first develop vision and mission statements and strategic plans before taking action, analogous to the notion of "ready, aim, fire." Instead, Fullan suggests that we adjust these actions to: "get ready," "fire," then "aim." First, it is useful to spend time reading current research about literacy theory and practice, and current policy issues that impact our practices as we "get ready." This background reading ensures that we know about and consider the challenges and pitfalls others have experienced as well as what is current in our field. Simultaneously, it is useful to begin to outline one's moral purpose and personal vision statement.

In sum, getting ready is important, but spending too much time in this activity can hold us back in our efforts. We also need to "fire," or engage in action and inquiry. Experimenting, trying new ideas, and adapting strategies and practices to our individual settings and students allows our "aim" to become sharper and better informed. We can create stronger personal and shared visions and new beliefs and practices through the process of inquiry. "Firing" also indicates holes in our knowledge base and the need for new information. This new knowledge may be critical to the "getting ready" strategies needed before gearing up to "fire" again.

Joe Ruhl offers the perfect example of "ready, fire, aim." He did not have a tried and true method, set of materials, or set of activities when he put his new learning system in place. Rather, he relied on a strong research base in teaching and learning, solid conceptual knowledge in biology, and effective ways to motivate students. It was through "firing" that Joe was able to see what worked well and respond to what was problematic. Through inquiry and reflection his aim became sharper and he was ready to "fire" yet again with new adaptations to his program.

Keeping the End in View: Responsive, Planful Teaching

As we talk about processes for understanding ourselves and the literacy needs of all learners, it is important to think about where we want to end up—What do we want our classrooms to look like? What do we want learners to be able to do? What does our pedagogy need to look like to support the needs of all learners? Dewey (1938/1981) calls this our "end in view." This "end," or goal, is informed by our moral purpose and vision, but it is more tangible: It is how the ideas are enacted. One pedagogy that matches the end in view we have explored thus far is called responsive, planful teaching.

Lee Galda, Bernice Cullinan, and Dorothy Strickland (1997) define *responsive teachers* as those individuals engaged in a pedagogy that allows them to teach "to the needs and abilities of students rather than to predetermined curriculum. A responsive teacher observes students and plans instruction accordingly. Responsive teachers are willing to alter plans to capitalize on a teachable moment" (p. 4). Responsive educators are also *planful* (Moje, 2000). Planful teachers go beyond planning (for example, making lists of activities, allocating time to events, or even connecting tasks with objectives in one's planbook). Instead, they "construct pedagogy that begins with the skills important to students' lives and that connects concepts to each other in coherent, systematic, and thoughtful ways" (p. 33).

As indicated in these definitions, responsive, planful teachers adhere to the notion that teaching, learning, and assessment are interconnected. Trevor Cairney (1995) describes this teaching/learning cycle as having several key components that are recursive in nature (see Figure 1). These components include planning, practice, evaluation, interpretation, and assessment—all of which impact students' learning. Cairney notes that the translation of assessment into planning and practice is dependent on the *theoretical knowledge* one has of language, learning styles, child development, culture and learning, and curricula; the *practical knowledge* one has of previous teaching experience, teaching strategies, resources, and school programs and policies; and the *particular knowledge of learners* including their knowledge and experience, interests, expectations, and school and cultural environment (p. 137). These knowledges will be explored throughout this book as well as other books in the Kids InSight series. As outlined previously, the particular knowledge of learners is a key focus of the series.

Reflection Point

Describe an example of responsive, planful teaching in your classroom. What are the challenges you face in enacting this type of pedagogy?

Figure 1
The Teaching and Learning Cycle

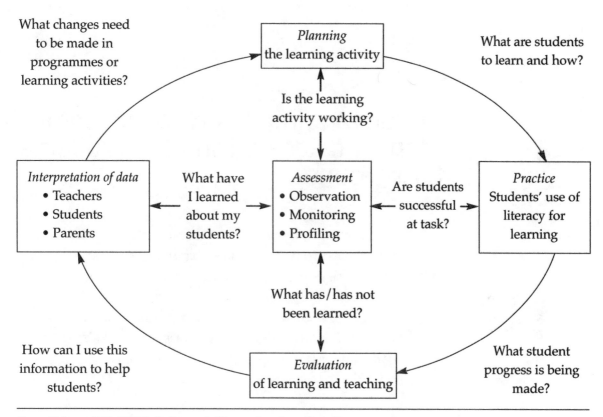

What changes need to be made in programmes or learning activities?

What are students to learn and how?

Planning
the learning activity

Is the learning activity working?

Interpretation of data
• Teachers
• Students
• Parents

What have I learned about my students?

Assessment
• Observation
• Monitoring
• Profiling

Are students successful at task?

Practice
Students' use of literacy for learning

What has/has not been learned?

How can I use this information to help students?

Evaluation
of learning and teaching

What student progress is being made?

From Cairney, T.H. (1995). *Pathways to literacy*. London: Cassell.

In the next chapter we explore our social and cultural backgrounds and those of our students as a way of understanding how our past experiences, cultural practices, and values shape how we view learners, our role as teachers, and events that unfold in our classrooms.

Chapter 3

Understanding Where We've Come From and Recognizing Our Students' Backgrounds

Recently my mother handed me a note I had written to her as a child. She had saved it. I think she valued the message and messenger, and wanted me to have it. The elaborately folded piece of notebook paper was addressed in red pencil "To: Mother." An additional note on the front read: "Please return pin to Debbie" (a piece of jewelry must have been used to hold the paper together so that the money, tucked away inside the note, wouldn't fall out). Inside, amidst many drawings of flowers, was the following message:

> *Dear Mother,*
>   *Here is the 77¢ plus 2¢ tax I owe you for the Eye-Lash Curler. I now have $9.00.*
>   *I have dusted my room so you will not have to. We can walk if it's nice! Luv, Debbie*
>   *PS. Have a nice day. You now have 79¢ to spend for yourself!"*

It brought tears to my eyes that my mom had kept this note—probably somewhere in her dresser—for 30 years. We laughed over the message because beyond the surface-level words of thanks hid a different purpose. What was it? I never cleaned my room or paid back money I owed without a reason! But one thing I did while growing up was a lot of writing and reading to learn about the world and to express my ideas and emotions. I assumed that everyone did the same and valued books and writing as much as I did. When I began to teach school, I realized that my cultural background—the experiences I'd had and things I valued—were often different from those of my students.

Excerpt from Deborah Dillon's literacy memoirs

Literacy Histories and Their Impact on Where We Are Headed

Many literacy professionals recognize and promote the writing of literacy histories or memoirs. William Zinsser (1987) noted in his book *Inventing the Truth: The Art and Craft of Memoir,* that a memoir is

> unlike an autobiography, which moves in a dutiful line from birth to fame, omitting nothing significant, [rather] the writer of a memoir takes us back to a corner of his or her life that was unusually vivid or intense.... [A] memoir is a window into a life. (p. 21)

Writing our literacy memoirs is an opportunity to understand social, cultural, and historical events in our pasts, as well as individuals and texts, that have influenced who we are today. As Bean (1998) notes in his work on secondary preservice teachers' literacy histories, these narratives serve as windows into teachers' beliefs and practices, many of which were formed very early in their own experiences in K–12 classrooms. Memoirs also provide a way for novice and practicing teachers to reflect on and potentially change practices (Graham, 1991). Our beliefs about learners, knowledge, and classroom practices strongly influence what and how we teach, and our past experiences and cultural backgrounds strongly shape our beliefs and practices. For example, many new teachers assume that their students' experiences in school will parallel their own experiences (Britzman, 1991).

Learning about our own literacy histories and the literacy experiences of our students is critical to meeting the needs of all learners. Take a few moments to respond to the questions in the Reflection Point that follows. These questions were taken from a "Reading and Writing Experiences" inventory my colleague David O'Brien and I developed with a group of professionals from the Lafayette, Indiana, School Corporation in 1996, and from an activity I designed with George Kamberelis in 1997 titled "Comparative Literacy Memoirs."

Reflection Point

Describe the literacy experiences you remember (a) at home prior to school and during your school years, (b) during your elementary school years, (c) during your middle school years, (d) during high school, (e) after high school to the present. Discuss individuals, places, and materials that are vivid in your mind. Identify positive and negative events and influences pertaining to your experiences. Use Calkins's (1994) advice: Describe the scene; make a particular picture and help us "see it" and understand its significance.

After reconstructing important literacy experiences and practices from your own life, informally interview someone from a field of study other than education (e.g., agriculture, music, engineering, medicine) with the intention of writing their literacy memoir. You can later compare and contrast his or her experiences with your own.

After you complete the questions above, list the similarities and differences between you and your interviewee. Reflect on how this comparative information affects your ideas about teaching and learning.

An Excerpt From a Literacy Memoir

Following is an excerpt from my literacy memoirs, which addresses the first question in the Reflection Point above. It outlines my experiences as a daughter and learner in K–16 settings. Following the memoir I present my analysis of this data source as one way, but certainly not the only way, to make sense of these data.

My parents valued education but believed that the teaching of reading and writing and other skills took place in school under the guidance of knowledgeable teachers and that books for reading could be found in the public and school libraries. Although we didn't have a lot of money for books at home, my parents bought us Little Golden Books and collections of Bible stories and Hans Christian Andersen fairy tales. My mom also saved points at a local grocery store to earn wild animal books with stickers that were colorful and very engaging. I have fond memories of my parents reading Bible stories to us from this large anthology each night before we went to sleep. I also remember our huge, special family Bible that my parents read from particularly at Christmas time. My sisters and I acted out the Christmas story using the figurines from the manger scene. We also created dramatic recreations of fairy tales and made-up stories, complete with costumes, scenery, and charges for audience members at holiday gatherings at my grandparents. My memories of writing included coloring in color books and writing thank-you notes and letters to relatives.

During my elementary school years I remember checking books out of the school library and reading them in bed early on Saturday mornings. I learned to read with the Dick and Jane series in first grade; I don't think I was reading prior to entering school. My scariest moments were round-robin reading sessions. I counted up the sentences to the one I knew I was to read and I don't remember what was read before or after my sentence. I did enjoy the reading skills workbooks we completed, working quickly to "race" with my seatmate. I enjoyed getting "A's" or "100%" on each page. A crisis point for me was my fifth-grade year when I moved mid-year to a new state and school and found that I was behind my classmates. My classmates thought I was weird and not very smart due to my southern accent and lack of ability to fit into their social groups and the routines already established in the classroom. My teacher, Mrs. Rupe, recognized that I was in trouble. She determined that I had the ability to do well in school, but I needed some transition support. She worked with me over the noon hour, during class, and after school to help me catch up on content and strategies that other kids already had and that I would need to succeed in class. Soon I was moving through the SRA reading kits, level-by-level with my peers. I didn't enjoy this form of reading (short texts with comprehension questions), but I wanted to be able to be like the other kids. I read every Nancy Drew and Hardy Boy series books I could get my hands on but I don't remember reading other forms of literature. I also don't remember much about my writing experiences except copying texts my teachers had written, doing handwriting and language exercises, and writing my autobiography in fifth or sixth grade.

As an adolescent, I read a lot of historical fiction, primarily during summer vacations. In school I enjoyed reading and memorizing the poetry of Byron and Shelly in my sophomore English class and writing my own poems. My English teacher motivated me to write about things I cared deeply about and she helped me believe that I was a good writer. I believed that I had the ability to write well until my freshman English professor shook this conception momentarily by giving me a "C" on my first paper in his class. However, what I came to learn from this teacher was how to write—that form and function are as important as ideas and passion. It took me awhile but I came to respect this professor because he challenged me, wrote comments on my papers, and talked with me about my work, instead of only recording a grade or "good job" at the top of my paper.

Currently I tend to read for work/school purposes, the newspaper, a few novels in the summer, health magazines and bulletins, books on how to raise a healthy baby, and children's books for two-year-olds. My writing ranges from personal notes, to e-mails, to research papers, to books. My ongoing goal is to find more time to read and write for my own personal development and reflection because I believe this will help me in all facets of my life.

Making Sense of Our Literacy Memoirs

In this analysis segment I model a strategy to use in making sense of your memoirs including organizing information to better see ideas, describing what you see, and interpreting what you see. This process allows you to revisit your memoirs and those of an individual you interviewed several times, and uncover new and deeper insights with each analysis of your writings. You may want to read the following directions to see how to analyze your literacy memoir, analyze your responses, and then compare your analysis with my findings.

1. Highlight or make a list of the following information as you reread your response to the first question: When and where did the majority of and/or most memorable literacy experiences occur? Identify positive and negative events by grade level or age level. Who participated in your literacy development—parents, teachers, peers?

2. Analyze your response to the first question: How did these experiences shape your motivations and goals at the time they occurred? Why were your literacy experiences positive or negative? Describe how you think your previous experiences have influenced your current ideas and practices in teaching literacy.

3. Repeat the highlighting and analysis strategies outlined here for your interviewee's memoirs. Then, compare and contrast the content contained in the two sets of memoirs. Think about what you learned and how this might affect your future teaching.

Here is an example of how I used the analysis strategy outlined in directions 1 and 2:

> *Description.* [Here is what I seem to be saying in my memoirs, using the analysis questions as a guide for making sense of my narrative.]

• When did my literacy experiences occur and where—in or out of school?

> Most of my formal literacy development occurred at school during my elementary years. I have some memories of writing development at the high school level but few memories of reading beyond fifth grade. At home my parents read to my sisters and me at night as an informal, family activity. Texts in my home included anthologies of stories, the Bible, small storybooks, and a few other print materials. Literacy events also included dramatic recreations of stories or oral texts.

• Positive and negative events by grade level or age level

> Positive events included most home experiences and most K–4 school experiences except for round-robin reading exercises. Less positive experiences occurred in fifth grade and college and these were tied to my low performance in comparison to the new contexts I found myself in. I don't have much recollection of reading and writing experiences during the middle grades.

• Who participated in my literacy development?

> My parents valued literacy but entrusted my formal education to teachers. My folks don't remember "teaching me to read or write" but encouraged me in my schoolwork and provided opportunities for me to obtain and read books (trips to the library) and reasons to write (e.g., letters, notes to relatives). Teachers, peers, and particular literacy events played a key role in my literacy development. Basal readers and round-robin reading formed the basis for my elementary reading instruction along with SRA kits and workbooks. I don't remember what most teachers did to support my instruction, but I learned to read and write and value these activities. My most vivid memories involve peers who made me feel competent and those who made me feel that I was not able to read

and write. My peers' actions may have been due to their perceptions about my social and cultural background and the difference between us.

Interpretation. [Here is what the experiences recounted in my memoirs seem to mean and how they might impact my beliefs and actions as a teacher.]

- How did these experiences shape my motivations and goals at the time they occurred?

For the most part I was highly motivated to learn to read and write. My parents supported my efforts and most of my teachers viewed me as a serious student and thus they valued my efforts. I generally liked school and wanted to succeed.

- Why were my literacy experiences positive or negative?

My negative fifth-grade experiences centered on differences between my cultural background and the backgrounds of students in my new class: I moved from the Appalachian area in Kentucky to Nebraska. While living in Kentucky I was immersed in the southern culture and language. When I moved, I entered a new culture in Nebraska and in the specific classroom I joined. Academic and social peer groups were already established; classroom routines were well known to all students and curriculum and assessments were familiar. All of these factors were new challenges for me, while I also coped with the loss of my friends and everything I had loved in Kentucky. Luckily, my new teacher saw something in me that others overlooked—she saw me as a person and sought ways to help me become part of the classroom community while also helping me develop the skills I lacked but needed to succeed in this setting. She couldn't make other kids like me but she provided me entrance into several activities and thus entry into particular peer groups. In a different way my college English professor provided me with feedback that helped me gain knowledge and strategies as a writer. I thought I already had that knowledge, but in reality I didn't. On the other hand, my high school teacher gave me the confidence and enthusiasm I needed to write but not the skills and strategies.

- How did my previous experiences influence my current definition of literacy?

In analyzing and reflecting on my memoirs, I have reconsidered several issues about literacy learners and my role as a teacher. I want to remember that each student in my classroom is an individual with a unique cultural background. I want to value and build on the experiences, knowledge, ways of expressing ideas, and interaction patterns each student brings to my classroom and support students' learning no matter where they are in their literacy development or what that development looks like. Further, I believe that caring about students isn't enough. For example, as a learner I wish more teachers had supported me affectively, cognitively, and emotionally throughout my literacy development (like Mrs. Rupe did).

I also have a different view of parents than I did before. Previously, I expected parents to do more to ensure that their children started school with appropriate literacy experiences. But these home experiences may look different than the ones I had or those I expect parents to provide. Some parents, similar to my own, may value literacy, reading to their children and having books in their homes, but defer the formal teaching of reading to those they consider to be "the experts"—teachers. I also will carefully consider the use of certain materials (SRA kits, workbooks) and activities (round-robin reading) and how these support or detract from students' literacy learning.

*Reflection Point*_____

Reflect on your literacy memoirs. How have your past experiences influenced the way you teach reading and writing?
What literacy practices do you value and expect students to display in your classroom? Using a critical lens, think about how your values might be influencing what you consider to be "good" versus "inappropriate" literacy practices from students.

Learning How to Understand the Literacy Histories and Cultural Backgrounds of Our Students

The analysis of a segment of my memoirs is one example of how you might make sense of your literacy memoirs; it shows how one's cultural background and life experiences affect beliefs and actions. Now let's consider how to couple this understanding of where you have been with where your students are coming from. First, what do you know about your students' past experiences in and out of school that have shaped who they are as literacy learners?

In working with Rick Umpleby and the learners in his basic-track English/reading class, I designed an interview guide to learn more about the students. Some sample instructions I gave students included the following:

- Describe yourself to me. Pretend that I know nothing about you.

(I followed this with a few probes to support students as they generated responses, but I tried not to ask leading questions. For example, I requested information about students' age, birthplace, where they were raised, what their family life was like, their mom and dad's jobs, descriptions of siblings, and the education levels/experiences of family members.)

- Describe your personal characteristics. How would others describe you?
- Describe your home life, your school life, and your outside social activities? What do you like to do? What do you do well?
- If I followed you around during a typical day, what are some of the things I would see and experience?
- What kinds of reading and writing experiences have you had? Were they positive or negative? Did they occur at home or school or both? Describe a few for me.
- What are your dreams for the future? What do you plan to do when you graduate?

I interviewed several students in Rick's class using these questions and a few others related to work in Rick's classroom. Most teachers do not have the time to use such a detailed interview guide with all students in their classes, especially if they teach middle school or high school. Thus, selecting a representative sample of students from a class is a useful strategy. In Rick's class of 16 students we chose a sample of three learners that included two females (one White and one Black) and one Black male. Although using this small sample was successful, I also would like to note that the times I have been able to interview *all* students in my classes, even through informal sessions before and after class or during free periods of time during the day, have resulted in a richer understanding of the individuals in my class. This has allowed me to connect with each and every student in a unique way that shapes everything we do together each day.

What follows is a segment from an interview I conducted with Yvonne, a Black female student in Rick Umpleby's class. You will encounter Yvonne throughout the rest of this book—this is just a brief introduction. Yvonne provided a window for me into a cultural background and literacy history very different from my own. From Yvonne I learned that a student who grows up in a home without a mother and father, and with few economic advantages and literacy materials, still values school, writing, reading, doing something interesting and important with her life, and striving to be a good person.

Yvonne came to school everyday in the same clean navy knit jacket, blouse or T-shirt, pair of blue jeans, and white tennis shoes. It seemed like these were the only clothes she had. As her teacher, Rick, noted, "The kids come from very poor homes—houses on stilts with windows out and 30 kids running around the yard in between the old broken down cars littering the landscape." This is exactly the scene that greeted me when I visited Yvonne at her home to talk about her life and future plans. During our talk together on her front porch, Yvonne described herself to me:

> I live with my grandma and her brother. I lived with my mom for a year—she had me and she left me. That was it. My mom was out on the streets; she was doing almost everything. And when I look at her, I say I'm not gonna be like her. I want to go to college in computers.... I'm considerate, I'm not a bragger, I care about other people, I don't care what they say about me, I will care about them. I don't like to hurt people's feelings; I care about all kinds of animals, bad, dangerous, or any kind. I feel that people should have a second chance or third chance.

Visiting Yvonne's home and listening to her talk about her family and her life as well as spending time with her at school both in and out of reading class helped me appreciate who she was—I gained insight into her and into her life. For example, Yvonne's comments remind me that there is so much more going on in learners' worlds than attending class and studying concepts and materials that teachers are excited about, and working on various tasks we believe to be helpful to the learning process. Students are individuals with hopes and dreams and lives inside and outside of school, with cognitive, affective, and emotional needs. We also learn about the influence of Yvonne's mother on her early and current life and her future goals. My inquiry into Yvonne's life, along with my observations of her interactions during classes at school, prompted me to read more about learners who have cultural backgrounds different from my own, students who are "distinguished by their ethnicity, social class, and/or language" (Au, 1993, p. 1). And this is important because as Au notes, a teacher's ability to understand and build on students' language patterns and literacy practices—particularly practices different from his or her own—is influenced by a teacher's own cultural background. What we also know is that teachers who are knowledgeable about students of diverse backgrounds are more likely to be responsive to these learners and adjust their pedagogy to meet their individual needs. (See Box 3-1 for a list of factors associated with children of diverse backgrounds.)

BOX 3-1
Factors Associated With Children of Diverse Backgrounds

ETHNICITY: determined by the national origin of one's ancestors; also reflects an ethnic groups' shared history, values, and behaviors (e.g., African American, Native American, Asian American, Hispanic American).

CLASS or socioeconomic status: indicators of class include parents' occupation and income; generally working class families or those living in poverty.

LANGUAGE: individuals for whom English is not their first language or they speak a nonmainstream variety of English (e.g., dialect); students who are bilingual or able to speak two languages.

From Au, K.H. (1993). *Literacy instruction in multicultural settings*. New York: Harcourt Brace.

Understanding the Cultural Backgrounds of Learners

While working with Yvonne and other children and adolescents in Georgia, I became interested in the work of Shirley Brice Heath (1982). Her long-term research findings indicate that children come to school from various social and cultural backgrounds with different learning styles or "ways of taking" from books and using language. As background, it would be useful to define the term *culture*, but there is no one definition. Au (1993), using the work of Hernandez (1990), defines culture as "a system of values, beliefs, and standards which guides people's thoughts, feelings, and behaviors" (p. 4). Au goes on to note that this system is complex; that culture is learned through interactions with others; that it is shared because members of a group construct common understandings; that it is influenced by and adapts to broader social and political conditions; and that it changes constantly. Understanding the many dimensions of culture, how it is constituted, and the influence it has on individuals and groups of people is key to gleaning insight about individual students and life in our classrooms.

In her landmark book, *Ways With Words: Language, Life, and Work in Communities and Classrooms* (1983), Heath studied three different communities in the southeastern United States to understand the influence of the home and community environment on the learning and language structures and use that children would be expected to employ in school settings. She found that families in the three communities differed dramatically in the ways language was used to socialize children and the patterns of language used within various literacy interactions.

For example, the children from the Maintown community learned ways of taking from books and materials at home that matched actions valued in school settings. These children, from both Black and White families, learned interaction routines from their parents for how to participate in literate activities; developed ways of connecting books and real-life experiences and displaying the skills they knew; and learned how to listen and wait for cues from others so they could show what they knew during classroom lessons.

In the other two communities, Trackton and Roadville, children representing different sociocultural groups learned to value other ways of talking and interacting and "taking" from books. For example, Trackton children grew up in large extended families in which parents were Black mill workers and sharecroppers. Children typically learned by trying various approaches (such as learning to talk). This occurred by listening to parents' conversations, chiming in or repeating chunks of language, and practicing literacy without intervention or direct teaching from parents. When children from Trackton homes went to school, they tended to face unfamiliar questioning routines and new patterns and rules of social interaction. In contrast, parents from Roadville, who were White and worked in the mills, felt it was important to teach their children "how to talk." This occurred when they helped their children learn rules about language and books that were then practiced, with parents coaching and rewarding children for their efforts. Children learned pieces of knowledge about books (such as letters, shapes, and colors) that were not contextualized nor connected to reality or to children's everyday experiences. These children experienced unfamiliar routines and patterns of interaction when they attended school.

In reflecting on Heath's research it is important to know that parents from all three communities valued education and wanted their children to do well in school. However, the children from Maintown were more likely to succeed in school because their literacy knowledge and practices, or "ways of knowing," more closely matched what schools and most teachers within schools value as appropriate literacy practices. This does not mean that these parents prepared their children to succeed in school and others did not. Rather, Heath's study makes visible to teachers the differences in language and culture children bring to school. By understanding children's ways of knowing, we can embrace these differences and adapt our pedagogy to better meet the needs of the variety of children who enter our classrooms. Adapting our pedagogy includes learning new ways to interact with students to ensure that alternative interaction patterns are offered to counter the more traditional school patterns (e.g., question and answer or recitation sessions). These traditional patterns may match our own ways of learning but do not necessarily match or support the learning styles of children from diverse backgrounds.

Understanding Context

At this point it is useful to stop and introduce an important concept that will reappear many times throughout this book and others in the Kids InSight series—*context*. Probably the most familiar use of this term for teachers is the idea of context clues in books, an aspect of the literacy process. However, this term also has been used by researchers to identify an event and to interpret actions within it (e.g., a read-aloud activity—what happens is described along with the room arrangement, who the participants are, their actions and reactions, and so on). However, this latter definition of context has been expanded in recent years (Rex, Green, Dixon, & Santa Barbara Classroom Discourse Group, 1998) to include the many contexts that individuals participate in each day and throughout their lives. For example, we are part of family contexts, peer group contexts, and community contexts. These various contexts shape who we are and what we do even when we are not immediately participating in them. As my colleagues and I have noted, "A context can be an event, a place, a social group, a realm of knowledge, or a moment in time" (Moje, Dillon, & O'Brien, 2000). Defining and understanding contexts is very important because contexts have important implications for the interpretation of particular texts, as well as for who learns what concepts and how learning occurs. This is clear when we think about the children from the three communities in Heath's study. Children were considered successful literacy learners in several contexts (bedtime reading sessions, home life in general, community activities) but not in others (school). How might we bridge these different knowledges, experiences, and contexts?

Building on the Cultural Backgrounds of Learners

To learn about the cultural backgrounds of students in Rick Umpleby's classroom, I interviewed Bernard, a Black male in the class. An example of Bernard's comments from this interview follows:

> I liked living with my grandfather—it was quiet and nicer. But when he died I had to move back home with my mother and father, my eight sisters, and my one brother. My dad was working at a wood craft busi-

ness—he ran the scales and helped the drivers unload logs. But he got laid off. My mom's trying to get a job running a sewing machine. I got a job helping the voc ag teacher—I mow the lawn around the school. I also play basketball. I stay away from home...when my parents start fussin' I just leave. If I don't play professional basketball I have many other skills such as a being a carpenter, painting, and more.

In examining Bernard's life we see that he came to school with particular values and experiences. He loved living with his grandfather, a person he admired and then missed greatly. He moved back in with a large family, so he comes to school with this background and knowledge as well. He also liked several content classes at the high school, including English/reading with Rick Umpleby. It appeared that Bernard brought a wealth of knowledge to school, comprised of unique and interesting family and community experiences, values, and practices.

Building on the work of Heath, researchers like Au and Kawakami (1995) and Nieto (1999) have noted that children come to school with "cultural capital" or values, behaviors, experiences, and tastes. These researchers urge educators to build on this "capital" or the ways of knowing that students bring to school. Nieto also cautions us to remember not to assume that all children from a particular background (such as Puerto Rican) are alike in what they know, how they learn, and what they need. (This is evident when we compare Bernard and Yvonne's backgrounds, experiences, and goals.) Rather, each child is an individual with a unique home life and particular interests and needs. Children represent bicultural backgrounds—for example, both Spanish and English.

While acknowledging cultural differences and building on students' cultural capital, educators also must create bridges between various cultures, including those of home and school. The teachers in Heath's study decided to use the cultural capital their students brought to school by designing a project in which parents and students became researchers. Families collected data on their literacy practices. The student researchers then recorded the practices, talked with parents about how they learned to talk and tell stories, and then presented the findings of their studies using conversation, drama, storytelling, and oral history formats. As teachers in the communities studied by Heath used these new teaching practices, they were working to help all students succeed.

However, as Luis Moll (1998), a Latino researcher, notes, the cultural capital and backgrounds that children bring to school are often not honored. In addition, Moll found that schools are settings where important resources of the culture (e.g., the critical, higher levels of knowledge needed to succeed) are or are not made available to students. For example, Moll and other researchers have found that students from working-class backgrounds receive more skill and drill type of instruction when compared to their typically White, affluent counterparts. This latter group usually engages in a more privileged form of instruction that is process oriented and in which teachers have high expectations for students' successful learning (Moll, 1998). Moll urges teachers to "confront a pedagogy of control" (p. 67), and to resist the political pressures to teach reading using a linear skills-based approach with an emphasis on phonics (to the exclusion of meaning) to children from working-class and language-diverse backgrounds. He does not devalue skills and strategies, but suggests that they be used to assist comprehension instruction. Above and beyond this message, Moll reminds us that schools are never neutral settings; rather, they are *political sites* because what occurs within them is always influenced by broader social, political, and economic factors from the outside.

Moll also focuses on expanding students' identities as learners by encouraging teachers to go beyond their classroom walls and out into homes and communities to understand the work and activities of members of various cultural settings—to understand a family's *funds of knowledge*. Funds of knowledge are "those bodies of knowledge that underlie household activities" (1998, p. 70). This includes how households function as part of the larger economy and how family members obtain and share material and intellectual resources through social interactions. Moll noted, for example, that households rarely operate alone—they network with other households to support each other economically and in distribution of labor. For example, often members of households have knowledge of child care, carpentry, and plumbing. Households share these funds as families work together to support each other in a community. Moll asserted that often educators assume that children from working-class homes— particularly homes where English is not the first language—have parents who have nothing to contribute to the learning of their children. Instead, it is our goal as educators to understand the cultural and social backgrounds of our students and build on students' funds of knowledge in the selection of curricula (e.g., topics of importance to the community) and activities (e.g., developing communities of learners like the households who work together). I found that Rick Umpleby was quite effective in doing this. He learned about his students' home and community contexts, selecting materials and activities to meet learners' interests and needs while still maintaining challenging content and meaningful learning.

A "Tension" in Views on Meeting the Needs of Linguistically and Culturally Diverse Students

To further complicate the issue of meeting the needs of all students, Black educator Lisa Delpit (1988) has argued that learners from diverse cultural and linguistic backgrounds, particularly poor children and children of color, require more than just progressive, process-oriented approaches to instruction. Why? Because Delpit believes that these process-oriented methodologies (such as whole language and process writing)—as enacted by many teachers—are not always effective in helping all children of color learn to read and write. Delpit does not reject the holistic, meaning-centered philosophies of process writing or whole language; rather, she believes that students of diverse backgrounds need effective instruction in both a skills-based and process-oriented approach to support their learning.

Delpit's ideas are affirmed by Maria de la Luz Reyes, a Chicana professor (a title she gives herself), who also believes that as educators rush to employ commendable practices such as process writing and whole language that they are often not prepared to make adaptations for linguistically different learners. The adaptations de la Luz Reyes (1992) identifies as necessary to ensure that language minority students benefit from process instruction include the need to change a "one size fits all" approach to instruction and the need to recognize that Hispanic students rely on and expect direct instructional intervention from the teacher in many instances because they view teachers as authority figures.

Important to the idea of crafting instruction that meets the needs of culturally diverse students is the concept of a *culture of power* (Delpit,

1988). What Delpit means by this term is that there are codes or rules that students need to know to succeed in classrooms or "participate in power." These include ways of talking, writing, dressing, and interacting with others. To be successful in school, Delpit maintains, is to acquire the culture of those in power (e.g., typically middle-class, White, English-speaking teachers). Delpit has generated five interwoven aspects of the culture of power:

1. Issues of power are enacted in classrooms.
2. There are codes or rules for participating in power; that is, there is a culture of power.
3. The rules of the culture of power are a reflection of the rules of the culture of those who have power.
4. If you are not already a participant in the culture of power, being told explicitly the rules of that culture makes acquiring power easier.
5. Those with power are frequently least aware of—or least willing to acknowledge—its existence. Those with less power are often most aware of its existence. (1988, p. 24)

The concept of a culture of power is not one that Delpit wants to exist, but she believes that it is typically the way things operate in schools. She suggests that

> students must be taught the codes needed to participate fully in the mainstream of American life, not by being forced to attend to hollow, inane, decontextualized subskills, but rather within the context of meaningful communicative endeavors; that they must be allowed the resource of the teacher's expert knowledge, while being helped to acknowledge their own "expertness" as well; and that even while students are assisted in learning the culture of power, they must also be helped to learn about the arbitrariness of those codes and about the power relationships they represent. (1988, p. 45)

In summary, the research of Heath, Au, de la Luz Reyes, Delpit, Moll, and Nieto focuses our attention on the cultural knowledge and practices students bring from home to school and reminds us that children do not enter school with deficits that place them at risk in their learning. Rather, learners bring "ways of knowing" that may be valued by teachers or not valued because they may or may not match our cultural backgrounds or traditional school practices. Honoring and building on students' cultural funds of knowledge, as well as teaching them the skills and knowledge they need to learn to read and write, are critical to developing successful and motivated learners. (See Box 3-2 for more resources on adjusting to the cultural differences of children.)

BOX 3-2
Recommended Reading on Adjusting to the Cultural Differences of Children

Au, K.H. (1993). *Literacy instruction in multicultural settings.* New York: Harcourt Brace.

de la Luz Reyes, M. (1992). Challenging vernable assumptions: Literacy instruction for linguistically different students. *Harvard Educational Review, 62*(4), 427–446.

Delpit, L.D. (1995). *Other people's children: Cultural conflict in the classroom.* New York: New Press. (This book includes papers from other publications: "Skills and other dilemmas of a progressive black educator," *Harvard Educational Review,* 1986; "The silenced dialogue: Power and pedagogy in educating other people's children," *Harvard Educational Review,* 1988.)

Gregory, E. (1995). What counts as reading: Children's views. In P. Murphy, M. Selinger, J. Bourne, & M. Briggs (Eds.), *Subject learning in the primary curriculum: Issues in English, sciences, and mathematics* (pp. 89–101). New York: Routledge.

Heath, S.B. (1983). *Ways with words: Language, life, and work in communities and classrooms.* New York: Cambridge University Press.

Ladson-Billings, G. (1994). *The dreamkeepers: Successful teachers of African American children.* San Francisco: Jossey-Bass.

Moll, L. (1998). Turning to the world: Bilingual schooling, literacy, and the cultural mediation of thinking. In T. Shanahan & F.V. Rodriguez-Brown (Eds.), *47th Yearbook of the National Reading Conference* (pp. 59–75). Chicago: National Reading Conference.

Nieto, S. (1999, December). *Language, literacy, and culture: Intersections and implications.* Presentation at the 49th Annual Meeting of the National Reading Conference, Orlando, FL.

Spangenberg-Urbschat, K., & Pritchard, R.H. (Ed.). (1994). *Kids come in all languages: Reading instruction for ESL students.* Newark, DE: International Reading Association.

Based on her findings from a study of successful teachers of African American students, Black educator Gloria Ladson-Billings (1994) identifies *culturally relevant practices* that affirm and strengthen students' cultural identities. Ladson-Billings defines culturally relevant teaching as "a pedagogy that empowers students intellectually, socially, emotionally, and politically by using cultural referents to impart knowledge, skills, and attitudes. These cultural referents are not merely vehicles for bridging or explaining the dominant culture; they are aspects of the curriculum in their own right" (pp. 17–18). First, culturally relevant teachers believe that all students—including those labeled at risk—can learn and achieve a level of excellence in their efforts. To promote excellence, teachers assume or share with students the responsibility for achieving excellence. For example, teachers function as conductors or charismatic teachers who take the lead in helping students learn, and coaches who partner with parents, community members, and students to help individuals achieve their respective "game plans." Second, culturally relevant teachers see themselves as part of the community and they desire to give back to this community. They also work to connect students with their respective cultural, racial, local, and global identities. Third, culturally relevant teachers develop strong relationships with students that extend beyond the classroom and they seek ways to help students connect with their peers in a community of learners. Fourth, culturally relevant teachers view the curriculum with a critical eye and look for ways to develop this same stance in students. These teachers also work to help students connect what they know with new concepts (scaffolding), and develop the skills and strategies needed to successfully construct knowledge and participate in literacy events. In sum, students who interact with culturally relevant teachers know that their home cultures are respected, they learn to understand the world, and they acquire the knowledge and critical stance needed to make a positive difference in the world.

Rick Umpleby is an example of a teacher who employs a culturally relevant pedagogy. I will present additional glimpses into his practices throughout the remainder of this book. But before moving on, pause for a moment and write responses in your journal to the questions in the following Reflection Point, then analyze your responses.

Reflection Point

Describe the social and cultural backgrounds of the students in your classroom. What cultural capital might these learners bring with them to school?

Talk to several students to learn about the literacies and funds of knowledge these learners bring from their homes and communities. How do you currently build on learners' "ways of knowing"? How do you help students learn the culture of power or school "ways of knowing"?

An Example of Culturally Relevant Practices and Meeting the Needs of Individual Learners

Yvonne often talked about Rick Umpleby and how he helped her learn and supported her as a person.

> He helped me a lot, he makes me want to work to give and do something. He show me that if I can do it in his class, I can get my grades up and do it in other classes. He makes school fun. I really wasn't interested in school, and you know if I'm not interested I'm not gonna do stuff. But he tells you in a friendly way that if you don't do this, you not gonna pass. Umpleby has his own style—he makes his own self. He teaches the way [from what] he learns. Umpleby wouldn't go into a class and say "this is the way we gonna do it." [He'd go into a class] and get into it—what they [students] like. He say "you draw?" and I say "yeah." And I'd show him some of my pictures and he'd say "that's real good." Umpleby's fun, he kinda act like one of us...he'll hang with us he talk with us. He really knows what the students like—he's funny, tells jokes, is crazy sometimes, and laughs with the class. He's great!
>
> [But] he'll tell us how it really is and if we have a little trouble [learning] he'll give us pointers. [This class] is different from anybody else's. Like he puts life into the characters—feeling and action. He got me into that book [*Of Mice and Men*]. At first it was boring but as he read it [aloud—the students followed along in their own copies] he got me into it...I understand it more now. He wouldn't say "Read the words" he'd help me and explain it [the story] to me. If I can get into it [the book], I'll read it. I came home and told Dar [her grandmother] the whole story about the two men

and their dream and how they cut the man [at the end] because he was re-
tarded. It [the story] was good.

Yvonne's story reveals how Rick developed powerful relationships
with students. He also gained insights from his observations of students'
lives in school and out of school, their interests, and their needs as learners. He built on the relationships he formed and the insights he gleaned
from students as he designed learning experiences with which students
connected. These experiences supported learners' cognitive, affective,
and social needs. For example, Yvonne wanted to pass the state Basic
Skills Test (BST) in reading and math, required to graduate from high
school and necessary to her dream of going on to school to learn about
computers. Rick provided "pointers" and some explicit instruction to help
students learn reading skills and strategies while at the same time enjoy
and understand what they were reading. He motivated students to believe
that they could learn while also arming them with the skills and information they needed to learn. Finally, he sought to match their social needs
by making learning safe and fun, using whole- and small-group formats
and using an unpredictable style of teaching and interacting with students. Yvonne described how Rick helped her learn how to read better
and how she found a story compelling, or as she said "good." The power
of Rick's teaching made such an impression on Yvonne that she shared
her learning with her primary caregiver, her grandmother.

In addition, Rick made it a point to learn as much as he could about
each of his students. He rode the bus with students, visited homes and
talked with parents, and coached students after school in sporting activities. He built on his students' interests and diverse backgrounds by encouraging them to use their cultural capital when learning to read and
write. For example, in response to Yvonne's desire to write about her life
and to examine how her experiences with her mother shaped who she
was, Rick used the context of writer's workshop. Students wrote in a journal each day and Yvonne wrote several pieces about her mother. Rick, recognizing the importance of the topic to Yvonne, supported her as she
crafted, revised, edited, and eventually published her poem about her
mom titled "Saddness" [sic].

Saddness
by Yvonne

Saddness is when you expect your
mother to come see you...
and she doesn't come.
Saddness is when it's your 16th birthday
And your mother doesn't come and
Later says she forgot.
Sadness is when you're always alone
When your mother leaves you by yourself.
Saddness is when you want to go outside
But it's beginning to rain.
Saddness is when a close relative dies
And you miss him or her very much
Saddness is wanting to help people
But you can't.
Saddness is wanting to be loved by your mother
But you aren't.

Yvonne's writing is clear, passionate, and represents a motivated learner who believes she is a writer. She also reveals a great deal about herself—freely—to her teacher and others. Rick celebrated Yvonne's work and urged her to continue writing about topics that were important to her, that were of interest, and that pushed her thinking. In sum, Rick Umpleby's role as a culturally responsive educator supported Yvonne's development as a reader and writer. I will provide more evidence for why I believe this to be true as we look closely into Rick's classroom and at other insightful teachers throughout this book.

Understanding our sociocultural backgrounds and those of our students is a powerful way to better meet the needs of all learners. (See Box 3-3 for tips on how to learn more about your students.) As the examples in this chapter indicate, students recognize and respond to teachers' efforts to understand their diverse backgrounds and bridge home, personal, and school practices. It can be as simple as making class fun for your students while helping them learn important skills, connect in meaningful ways to literature, and explore their emotions and dreams through dis-

---

BOX 3-3
Learn More About Your Students

1. Select three students that you consider to be representative of the range of students in your class (various cultural, social, ethnic, and academic backgrounds; boys and girls).
2. Use an interest/motivational survey or interview guide and collect data from selected students to learn more about their life and academic histories.
3. Analyze each student's responses to the questions. Write a statement describing what you learned about each student. Synthesize patterns you see across students' responses. What patterns do you see? Are there frequency patterns associated with particular responses?
4. What did you find surprising in the results? What challenges do you see, or what issues need to be resolved to help you meet the interests and motivational needs of students and support them as learners?

---

cussions and writings. Yvonne reminds us that it is important for teachers to look beyond the labels applied to kids such as "low readers" and "at risk" to see what learners can do, and to uncover the wonderful talents that reside within these students.

Chapter 4

Identifying Beliefs and Knowledge, Uncovering Tensions, and Solving Problems

*I think my teacher is really good—the best I've had, and I like
group work, but I believe that sometimes we work alone too much. I
mean in the group. And there's not enough attention to helping us learn
because sometimes it's...the stuff is really hard. A teacher needs to be
there...to tell you what to do.*

*Interview with Jay, a male student in a science class
at Jefferson High School*

laire, a biology teacher in the Lafayette School Corporation
(LSC), and a participant in a professional development seminar
that I facilitated, reflected on her beliefs about literacy, her challenges in teaching, and what her students told her were their challenges
to learning in her classroom. The student comments caused Claire to begin to question her beliefs about learning and the role of literacy in her
classroom. Claire related the following in her reflection journal:

> I believe that literacy is the ability to read texts and comprehend
> them. I don't teach literacy, but students do read to learn science; they also
> use study guides and lab sheets to guide small-group learning; and the
> textbook is one resource. My biggest challenges as a teacher are relating
> meaningful information, encouraging students to "risk" an inference,
> encouraging the realization in students that they have useful prior knowl-
> edge, and helping students read comprehensively. The way I support stu-

dents' learning is by preparing study guides and helping students learn important vocabulary. I don't assess literacy.

Claire designed a questionnaire that asked her students to detail what was hard about learning science in her classroom. She also observed her students working in groups and recorded observation notes. She then videotaped a class lesson. The following is her written analysis of these data.

> The students in my class identified the following as the biggest challenge: seeing a meaningful application of science to their lives. This is one of my biggest goals—something I believed I was doing well. Students also said they needed help determining important facts within a text, connecting one concept to another, linking prior knowledge to new knowledge, making inferences, and learning scientific vocabulary. I guess I thought that the small-group work would motivate the students and they could support each others' learning. But it appears that some explicit instruction from me is important on certain concepts. And I used to believe that it wasn't necessary to teach literacy skills and strategies to students. But I see that there are content-specific ways of learning science that necessitate my developing strategies to help kids understand the ideas. I won't be teaching kids how to read and write but how to use these tools to make sense of science concepts.

Donna, also a participant in the professional development seminar, is a high school mathematics teacher in LSC. She teaches intensive math, algebra, calculus, and precalculus. In a reflective paper Donna wrote, where she outlines her beliefs about learning, literacy, and mathematics, she states that literacy is the ability to use oral language, reading, and writing to learn math concepts. She struggles with the fact that reading texts in calculus is hard.

> I believe that the readability level in mathematics is much higher and the concepts are more difficult to understand [than other subject areas]. I have become very good at being the total text for the students in these classes. I can explain the material in a way that is easily understood. But I don't believe that this way of teaching is best for students. I am really struggling with how to use reading to learn. And what is my role in the learning process? Also, I want to learn more about the use of writing and math. I am not a good writer and I do not enjoy the process of writing but I understand as a teacher that writing can be a powerful learning tool. I also believe that discussions are helpful in developing students' oral language and as a result, students' mathematical understanding. I just am not comfortable with the large-group discussion format but I have been trying out small-group discussions. These seem to work well.

How Do Our Beliefs and Knowledge Base Affect Our Practices?

In the excerpts from reflection documents presented here we can see how pedagogy is influenced by a teacher's belief system and knowledge base (theory and research findings) about learning, literacy, and the role of students and teachers as they work together in classrooms. Pedagogy is also shaped by our practices. When we articulate and examine our beliefs, knowledge base, and practices we often sift out discrepancies that are grounded in beliefs that we have adhered to but may not have a rationale for, or which may occur due to gaps in our knowledge base. Add to this the fact that students have their own beliefs about particular teaching practices that they think support their learning. It is a complex set of often conflicting ideas within which teachers have to make sense of their pedagogy.

For example, Claire believes that literacy is the ability to read and comprehend what one has read. She has students use study guides, lab sheets, and the textbook to learn science concepts. As a way to motivate students in her class, Claire allows them to work in small groups to help support one another's learning. If we look closely at what Claire said, however, we see that to her, literacy is more than reading and comprehending; it is talking and writing to make sense of ideas, and reading multiple texts including texts the teacher and other students have created.

Conflicting information also emerges for Claire after she gives her students a questionnaire designed to potentially reaffirm many of her current practices and allow her to fine-tune a few things that were not working. Instead, as she writes in her reflection journal, her belief that she has made science meaningful for students is shaken deeply. Students do not seem to see how science applies to their lives. Claire's practice of creating study guides to help students better understand concepts also is questioned when students responded that they want more explicit instruction from their teacher. In addition, Claire used to believe that it was not necessary for her to teach literacy (reading), but after polling her students she has decided that some content-specific literacy strategies might be useful in helping the class better understand science concepts. But she is unsure about what literacy strategies would work best for her students and which ones would match her content goals. She recognizes a gap in her knowledge base.

Donna defines literacy as the ability to use oral language, reading, and writing to learn a particular subject area, but she struggles with how to teach students to read a calculus text, which she considers "hard" due to concept load and readability. She relates that she has compensated for the difficulty of the text and her lack of strategies to help students make sense of it by becoming "the total text" for her class (e.g., she is the reservoir of knowledge). In analyzing her reflections, we can see that Donna realizes that serving as the text may support students in the short run, but this approach does not serve them well in the long run. There is also a discrepancy between her acknowledged need to help her class use literacy as a tool in mathematics class, and her lack of knowledge for how to use reading, writing, and discussion to support students' learning. Claire and Donna illustrate how important a teacher's knowledge base and beliefs are to students' learning. We also see how intertwined these two components are.

Why Is Knowledge Important to Teachers?

Knowledge is in the minds of individual learners and is defined as a cognitive outcome of thought, based on objective facts. Theorists believe that learners construct knowledge in an active manner and that learning occurs through social interactions in which language and literacy are used to convey and construct thoughts. The teacher's role is often defined as providing numerous opportunities for students to talk about ideas and ways of making sense of new information, and guiding students' constructions of particular concepts. Some researchers have described knowledge as a schematically organized set of structures; others have classified knowledge as *declarative* (knowledge of what), *procedural* (knowledge of how), and *conditional* (knowledge of when and why). For example, declarative knowledge would be knowledge about reading processes. Procedural knowledge is associated with how particular approaches and strategies might be used to help students learn to read. Conditional knowledge is one's ability to know when to use a particular strategy over another one in certain situations and why this strategy is more effective in supporting learners' needs. The concept of knowledge construction is linked closely to learning—an idea we will explore in more detail.

Why Are Beliefs Important to Teachers?

Beliefs are based on evaluation, judgment, and affective response (see Ernest, 1989; Nisbitt & Ross, 1980 for further discussion of these ideas). Beliefs also are based on past experiences (either an intense experience or a succession of events in one's life), our knowledge base (knowledge of content and pedagogical knowledge or ways to teach content), and daily work with students or practices (such as our actions that confirm or test our beliefs). Beliefs are deeply personal and are thought to have more of an impact on a teacher's actions than his or her knowledge base does—in fact, they sometimes operate independently of knowledge (Nespor, 1987; Pajares, 1992). Ultimately, beliefs indicate the decisions we will make in our practice and the actions we will take (Bandura, 1986; Nisbitt & Ross, 1980), combined with other factors (such as institutional constraints).

Beliefs also are often resistant to change even in the face of new or disconfirming evidence. This is because beliefs are so much a part of the fabric of our beings. As Dorothy Watson (1994) notes, "We are our beliefs. They direct everything that happens in or out of our classrooms. Beliefs, as a heuristic or driving force, must be articulated and held up for ourselves and other to see" (p. 606). In fact, shifts in beliefs do occur as a result of closely examining our thoughts to determine how and why the beliefs were formed initially. Shifts also occur when we continually test beliefs by reading new information, observing ourselves and other teachers and students in action, and experiencing and reflecting on events that cause us to question previously held ideas. I encourage you to use your journal to detail your beliefs about teaching, learning, and literacy to provide a starting point in dealing with the challenges you face in meeting all students' needs.

*Reflection Point*_____

What is your definition of *learning*—how do you believe kids learn? What is your definition of *literacy*?

How do you believe kids learn to read and write? How do they continue to develop their reading and writing abilities in upper elementary school, middle school, and high school?

What role do you assume in helping students develop their reading and writing abilities? What role do students play in this process? How do you assess students' literacy learning and what tools do you use?

What Do Our Beliefs Reveal?

As you review your responses to this Reflection Point, what do you feel strongly about in terms of your beliefs about teaching, learning, and literacy processes? What components of your knowledge base are strong? Which require more strengthening? What would you like to know more about? Comparing other colleagues' responses to the questions in the Reflection Point with your own and engaging in dialogue about the similarities and differences in responses is a useful activity to engage in to understand your beliefs and knowledge. For example, in responding to the questions, How do kids learn and what is the role of the learner?, teachers from one LSC elementary school individually recorded responses, shared ideas and grappled with different points of view, and then constructed the following list:

- Learning is natural; all students can learn; it is a personal and inner process that involves making connections to or integrating what one already knows or has experienced to construct new understandings.
- Language is fundamental to the process of meaning construction, and learning takes place most often through social interactions.
- Learning is developmental and occurs over a lifetime.
- Learners should be actively engaged participants, self-disciplined, creative, and motivated.
- Learners should have choice in what they learn and take responsibility for their own learning.
- Learners should be involved in evaluating their own work.

The teachers also responded to the question, What role do teachers play in the learning process? Respondents stated that teaching is a natural process of giving and sharing what one knows with others as well as learning from learners. Teachers were characterized as "students" who learn from learners, yet are "more knowledgeable others" and serve as mentors and role models. Teachers also were identified as observing and assessing students' progress and making decisions based on this information. The following is a synthesis of LSC teachers' responses to the question.

Educators should

- provide students with interesting and engaging opportunities to make sense of their world by exploring ideas with others in creative ways so that children experience success;
- provide a climate for learning that is communicative, just, disciplined, and caring;
- encourage choice, risk taking, modeling, and success; encourage students to have high expectations of themselves; and
- select appropriate materials and activities and have a wealth of diverse strategies to support the learning of all students.

Let's look closely at these responses to understand what these teachers believe. Generally the teachers indicated that learning is an individual cognitive process and that students construct meaning through social interactions. These teachers also believe that all students can learn, that learning is a developmental process, and that the process may look different and unfold differently for each child. They also indicated that the responsibility for learning resides in the learner—that a person makes connections and integrates new knowledge with the known. They also see learners as needing to display self-discipline, responsibility, creativity, and motivation as they learn; they noted that learners also need to be provided with choice in tasks and ownership in evaluating what they learn.

The LSC teachers believe their role is "the more knowledgeable other" who guides the learning of students and evaluates that learning. Teachers believe that students must take responsibility for their learning, but they also acknowledge that the teacher has to provide an environment conducive to learning, along with a variety of activities, materials, and strategies that support each learner's development. The teachers indicated a desire to be caring toward students yet provide a context that is just and disciplined. Communication between teachers and students is important. Overall, the creation of classroom contexts with conditions that enable learning are necessary for effective teaching and learning to occur. Further, teachers and students each have roles and responsibilities necessary in supporting learning processes. Finally, a wealth of materials, activities, and strategies are needed to help learners develop cognitively and affectively.

The following Reflection Point is designed for you to describe where you are currently in your practices. The best data collected are those that are complete and forthright. Although we often want to record what we would like to believe or what we think we ought to be doing in our classrooms, it is much more useful to document the "good, bad, beautiful, and the ugly" associated with our classroom practices and beliefs.

Reflection Point_____

Select a typical day or week in your classroom. Keep notes about your planning process (why you selected and organized particular activities in certain ways) and what occurred during the day (interactions with students, a description of how events unfolded). Second, audiotape one class period or a particular literacy lesson. Third, listen to the tape, taking informal notes that outline what happened during the lesson and what you learned about how and what students learned and the literacy practices in which they engaged.

Take the data collected and write a description of a typical day in your classroom. Detail what literacy teaching and learning looks like and the events that occur. What does students' learning look like in practice? What does literacy look like in practice? How do the definitions you construct from your observations compare to the definitions of *learning* and *literacy* you generated in the Reflection Point earlier in the chapter?

In the next section of the chapter we will turn inward again to examine discrepancies that emerge when theories or practices clash with previous experiences or beliefs, or when inquiry and reflection on practices illuminate a problematic situation. Specifically, we will examine our beliefs about how students learn and teachers teach, and how students learn to read and write and how teachers support these processes. We also will look at the classroom conditions necessary to support students' learning.

Dealing With Tensions in Our Practices

Rick Umpleby spent a considerable amount of time each week reflecting on how to motivate and support the learning of students like Yvonne (introduced in Chapter 1 and discussed at length in Chapter 3). He searched for activities to meet her needs as a person and as a learner. For example, he used the lyrics of a Marvin Gaye song as a springboard for a writing assignment about heroes. The students loved listening to the music—twice in one class period—and left the room humming and talking about the cool lesson they had just participated in. When I talked with Rick about his students, he was always quick to point out the challenges he faced as a teacher.

> My weakness is probably discipline. I don't keep kids as rigidly as most folks would like me to—like alphabetical seating and stuff. I let them talk out in class and let them joan me [tease in a fun, sarcastic manner] the last 5 minutes of class when we're finished with work. I tend to make work too interesting for the kids—you know some teachers have a rationalization for some of their materials being boring saying "Hey, life ain't no bowl of cherries—you're [students] gonna have to do things you don't like to do." And this is the truth. [But] I tend to shy away from things that I know are going to bore the kids. I work to help them follow through on something and help them find the redeeming value in things they are fascinated in. Also, maybe I trust kids too much—I get burned at it every year. I let some kid out of class for a bit and he gets in trouble...maybe I'm image-conscious and want administrators and others to know that I have my finger on things. But maybe my overall weakness is that I just get too involved with kids—too friendly. Even though they know that once the bell rings it's time to work.

As noted in these comments, a teacher's beliefs about learners and the learning process can create tensions and problems that affect how a teacher works to support learners' needs. According to *Webster's Dictio-*

nary, tensions are stress points when two balancing forces cause extension, and they are pressures when one has an inner striving, unrest or imbalance. *Problems*, on the other hand, are questions raised for inquiry or consideration. Thus, tensions between beliefs, practices, peers' opinions, and research findings all provide opportunities for inquiry. For example, a tension for Rick was the way his peers viewed his teaching practices—they thought he was too easy on his students, stating that he "spoon-fed" them by reading aloud to them or allowing them to work together on assignments. Several colleagues felt that Rick should stick to teaching the low-track students in his classroom the basic skills they needed to pass the skills test to enable them to exit high school. Several peers found his teaching style "loose" and lacking in discipline because he talked with students in an informal manner (joaning) and allowed them to call out answers in class. Rick was being pulled in two directions by two competing value systems. He felt the need to design motivating lessons and provide a pedagogy in which all students could succeed, yet he also recognized the need to help students become successful in environments outside his classroom. This tension formed the basis of Rick's inquiry problem.

First, Rick carefully assessed his students' needs and developed ways to support them and motivate their learning. He also engaged in personal inquiry projects to improve his practice, such as studying his patterns of interactions with students during discussions about reading assignments. And he consulted research literature to see if there was a sound rationale for his actions or a reason to adjust his practices. Finally, he was able to clearly articulate the reasons undergirding his choice of materials and activities and his actions. Despite challenges from colleagues and administrators, and occasional moments of self-doubt, he had a clear moral purpose and a vision that guided his actions. But the tensions Rick identified continued to be points of reflection, inquiry, and in some cases change in practice.

Problems are pervasive in our work as teachers and have often been viewed as a negative force. In reality we can use problems to our benefit to renew our practices and create exciting and meaningful classrooms. The brighter side of problems are detailed in the following section.

"Problems Are Our Friends"

Fullan (1993) indicates that renewal efforts typically fail for two basic reasons: Problems are "complex and intractable" and "workable, powerful solutions are hard to conceive and even harder to put into practice." Second, the strategies that educators use to renew their actions often do not focus on things that will really make a difference. This is because educators fail to address "fundamental instructional renewal" or the "development of new collaborative cultures among educators" (p. 46).

Fullan cites the need for a new paradigm of change, grounded in eight basic lessons:

> 1. You can't mandate what matters—the more complex the change the less you can force it;
>
> 2. Change is a journey not a blueprint—change is nonlinear, loaded with uncertainty and excitement and sometimes perverse;
>
> 3. Problems are our friends—problems are inevitable and you can't learn without them;
>
> 4. Vision and strategic planning come later—premature visions and planning blind;
>
> 5. Individualism and collectivism must have equal power—there are no one-sided solutions to isolation and groupthink;
>
> 6. Neither centralization nor decentralization works—both top-down and bottom-up strategies are necessary;
>
> 7. Connections with the wider environment is critical for success—the best organizations learn externally as well as internally;
>
> 8. Every person is a change agent—change is too important to leave to the experts, personal mind set and mastery is the ultimate protection. (pp. 21–22)

Fullan's third statement deserves closer inspection:

> Problems are our friends...[or] conflict is essential to any successful change effort.... We cannot develop effective responses to complex situations unless we actively seek and confront the real problems which are, in fact, difficult to solve.... It is only through immersing ourselves in problems that we can come up with creative solutions. (1993, pp. 26–27)

Solving complex educational problems requires special skills and strategies that many teachers have yet to develop. For example, how many of us take the time to track our progress in solving problems in an ongoing fashion, building in time to think about what we have done and learned and how this information might help us anticipate what action we need to take in the future? In addition, once problems are identified and we work to reconsider our practices, how many of us sit down and identify the reasons why problems existed or surfaced in the first place? It is through asking and solving these deeper issues that successful educators move forward in their work.

Often conflicts and disagreements arise among colleagues when tensions surface. However, many educators, in an attempt to "get along," do not probe, disagree, and question their colleagues' ideas and actions because this might be viewed as nonparticipatory and destructive. In reality, serving as a "critical friend" helps to move tensions toward problem formulation. Problem-solving processes also are moved forward. Openness, risk taking, inquiry, and conflict are essential. Of course, as Fullan notes, problems are our friends only if we do something about them.

Tensions associated with literacy learning, teaching, and assessment surround us daily—in our classrooms and communities, in the privacy of our homes, and in political arenas. Teachers are often caught between several tensions as they work to meet the literacy needs of all students in their classrooms. To move forward, we must acknowledge these tensions, define them as problems for inquiry, consider which problems are important to solve, and create plans to solve them. I invite readers to pause for a moment and write a response in your journal to the following questions, then analyze your responses before moving on to the next section of the chapter.

Reflection Point

What tensions do you currently face when working to meet the literacy needs of your students? Do your colleagues face similar tensions in their work? Initiate a conversation about these tensions. Working with your colleagues, begin to define selected tensions as problems for inquiry.

Tensions Facing Literacy Educators

David O'Brien and I asked the first question from this Reflection Point to our colleagues from LSC. Following, I share a sampling of the written responses to this question about tensions. Many educators may identify with these ideas.

> I am torn between using a phonics-based approach and a more holistic, literature-based approach. My kids need both but can the two approaches/philosophies coexist? Plus, I am held accountable for the kids' scores on the standardized tests.
>
> Janice (second-grade teacher)

> I am confused about whether I should ditch my basal and buy tradebooks because everyone seems to be going to a literature-based approach. I don't know what literature to use or the best ways to teach with books.
>
> Marlene (fifth-grade teacher)

> I used to think I was a whole language teacher but I think I need to reconsider and move towards a balanced approach—what does this mean for my practice?
>
> Becky (first-grade teacher)

> I know that explicit and often sequenced instruction of skills and strategies is important but how do I resolve the need for guided/facilitated learning that focuses on meaning?
>
> Nancy (resource room)

> I think that thematic instruction is better than separate subjects but how do I ensure that kids learn the important concepts they need in math and science as well as the skills and strategies they need as readers and writers?
>
> Jennifer (fourth-grade teacher)

As a research group we examined the concerns expressed by individuals and patterns that emerged across the group. As background, this group of K–5 teachers had just moved from a more traditional basal program to a literature-based approach to teaching reading. Teachers were working in teams to select books to use at each grade level. Some grades used a thematic approach (e.g., a unit on the rain forest) while others used genre, author, or classic literature selections as their organizing thread. As the teachers moved away from the basal they found it necessary to articulate to one another (and parents) what word recognition and comprehension skills they would be covering and what this instruction would look like using trade books instead of the basal. Due to concerns about preparing students appropriately and helping them succeed on the state proficiency exam, several teachers adhered to their previous teaching practices, such as using a phonics workbook to explicitly teach phonics, a practice separate from reading literature and talking about it in response groups. Other teachers created comprehension questions, much like those found in traditional basals, for use in guiding literature circle discussions.

Through our discussion a number of tensions arose for teachers about how students learn, how they learn to read and write, what approaches work best to support students' learning, and the constraints teachers felt (e.g., test scores) when making instructional decisions. As tensions surfaced and were articulated, they became the basis for conversations, and teachers found that they were not alone in their concerns. The teachers developed inquiry questions both individually and collaboratively in an attempt to address these tensions. As a school, they worked in teams to address literacy issues, seeking coherence and continuity in philosophy and approaches to best meet the needs of their K–5 students.

Middle school and high school teachers from LSC also expressed tensions:

> I understand the reason that all teachers should be concerned about helping kids improve their reading and writing abilities but I already have so little time to cover content. And I have over 125 students in 5 class periods—I have trouble determining how to meet the needs of all kids. Right now I'm trying to figure out how to use the Internet with my students and other forms of technology. I don't even know much about technology.
>
> John (science)

> I don't see how literacy is important to my content area because we don't deal with textbooks.
>
> Sue (art)

> I see my colleagues just following the steps of reading and writing workshop approaches but it isn't a linear process. I see a lot of kids slipping through the cracks because they are asked to read books they can't connect with or write about topics they have no interest in. But then some kids write about taboo subjects and how do we deal with this? And conferencing with kids—this is a real challenge!
>
> Joy (English)

> We have a pretty rigid departmental focus on teaching and learning
> content and little interest in integrating content (like math and literacy)
> or working in cross-content area teams (like math, literacy, and science).
> I want to learn how to do this because I think kids would benefit, but
> how do I get around the way my school is structured?
>
> Donna (math)

As a research group we looked at the responses each person had written and found concerns with the numbers of students taught each day and the difficulties in working within the secondary school setting (departmental focus, content specializations). There was also the prevailing idea that literacy skills (reading and writing) are under the purview of the English and reading teachers and thus are not the concern of content area teachers. This is because many subjects do not use textbooks (art, music) or believe that they should not rely on textbooks (for example, in science and math, hands-on problem-solving or discovery learning is promoted). Yet most of the teachers noted that their students had difficulties reading about topics in their classes and articulating their knowledge via writing, talking, or other ways of showing knowledge.

Concerns also were raised about approaches considered fairly progressive such as process writing. Teachers were critically examining what worked for students within a program and what did not, they acknowledged challenging problems like organizing time to conference and using this time effectively, and they identified the challenge of meeting students' cognitive and affective needs. Writing, sharing concerns, and reflecting on practices that work and do not work are key ways to solve problems. Participants who engage in these activities gain new ideas, the benefits of belonging to a community of learners, and the motivation to carry on with interesting and challenging work.

An Interactive and Integrative Model of Thinking About Beliefs, Knowledge, and Practice

A model that offers an excellent way to think about the role of beliefs, practice, research, and inquiry was developed by Jan Turbill, a literacy researcher from Australia, and her colleagues (Turbill, Butler,

Cambourne, & Langton, 1991, 1993). These scholars developed a staff development program called "Frameworks" that consists of four basic domains of knowledge and understandings that help teachers change the learning culture of a school. These domains include My Personal Theory, My Personal Theory in Practice, Theory of Others, and Theory of Others in Practice. The overall goal is for teachers to view themselves as perpetual learners. Turbill and her colleagues intend to help teachers shift their practices through the interaction of the four domains or the testing of personal theory. This is accomplished by asking participants to examine their practices and the practices of others as well as reading, reflecting, sharing ideas, and collaborating with colleagues.

What is unique about the Frameworks model is the focus on asking teachers to think about learning processes and their students as learners while they concurrently think about the strategies and processes that they (teachers) use as learners. Working through questions such as What is learning? and How do I learn? helps teachers make explicit their tacit knowledge. In addition, asking teachers to compare what they believe with what they actually do in practice, along with studying the research literature and others' practices, challenges an individual's thinking and beliefs or creates what Turbill calls "intellectual unrest" (p. 6). In our work with LSC educators, David O'Brien and I have discovered that when teachers put forth their beliefs, inquire into and describe their practices, and articulate *why* they engage in the practices that they do, then they can reconsider their practices and realize changes in teaching and learning.

Analyzing Tensions and Engaging in Inquiry

Issues confronting educators in LSC (see Box 4-1 on page 88) are very similar to those expressed by teachers in K–12 as well as university and other educational settings internationally. As we examine these tensions, it is important to acknowledge the various educational, societal, and political influences that pose challenges within our work, yet not allow these issues to divert our attention from a focus on individual students and the practices that support learners' development. As I learned from working with my LSC colleagues, acknowledging tensions requires that we first identify and write about these issues—describing situations and examples clearly for others and ourselves. Second, we need to engage in inquiry or problem solving in which we look closely at our actions and our thoughts and beliefs, and ask hard questions of ourselves.

BOX 4-1
Tensions That Arise for K–12 Educators

- There are new and multiple definitions of literacy, yet I only know about more traditional definitions of reading, writing, listening, and speaking.
- There are various purposes for, and kinds of, reading and writing (to glean facts, literary aspects, aesthetic, interpreting, connecting), yet I am only familiar with reading to gain information and writing to provide information.
- There are new forms of texts (genres) and the need for balance and diversity of electronic and print materials and other forms of texts (art work), yet I only know how to teach from a single textbook.
- There is a need for multiple interpretations of texts and opportunities to respond, yet I fall into a pattern of requesting one answer that must be given in one particular format.
- There is a need to infuse technology and the Internet into my teaching, but I am unsure as to how to do this and how to merge technology with the use of more traditional texts and forms of instruction.
- There is a push for structured, step-by-step instruction, yet I want to move toward more responsive, planful pedagogy to better meet students' learning needs.
- There is a need to cover content, yet I want to focus on helping students learn a few concepts well.
- There is a need for both explicit instruction and facilitated or guided teaching, yet I am unsure as to when I should use each type of instruction.
- There is a need to meet each student's needs, yet I am unsure about how to move away from a "one size fits all" or "aiming for the average student" position.
- There is a concern for what information we can or should obtain in order to meet each student's needs versus finding new ways to understand each student's family and academic history.
- There are calls for standards and accountability to drive what I teach and what learning looks like, yet I want to meet individual student's needs in interesting as well as intellectual ways, grounding my efforts upon standards.
- There is a concern that standardized tests drive instruction, yet authentic, performance-based assessments and portfolios with benchmarks for learning guiding pedagogical efforts seem to be better ways to document what students know and can do.

(Taken from LSC teacher questionaires)

Moving From Tensions to Inquiry Problems: An Example

What follows is an example of a teaching tension I identified and then shaped into an inquiry problem. My tension emerged when my belief about the need to guide students' learning in my elementary literacy course conflicted with my students' beliefs about strategies that helped them learn course content. Specifically, I developed reading guides for various articles and book chapters we were reading. I created questions to help students sort out important concepts and practice articulating ideas. I believed that this activity would help students actively construct knowledge as they read, and help them come to class prepared to talk about what they had learned along with questions they still had about concepts. I was disappointed to learn that students thought that the reading guides were not helpful.

I sat at my desk and wrote about the tension that emerged for me between my beliefs, the knowledge base I had about how students learn, and what occurred in practice with this group of students. For example, I described instances when I had not developed guides to help students focus on key ideas and they did not seem prepared for discussions. Instead, my students relied on me to tell them the key ideas from the text. I described why I developed the guides, and described putting the guides into practice and the students' finding that the strategy was not effective. I speculated why they believed as they did. Then I formed a problem statement and designed an inquiry project to understand and find answers to the problem. My problem statement, written in the form of a question, was, What are students' perspectives about how to learn course content in meaningful ways where they can write and talk about the ideas they are constructing? To address this question I decided to collect several forms of data. First, I met with small groups of students during class. I asked them to tell me about the guides—how they used them, what was and was not helpful. I queried them about a better solution that might address their needs as well as mine. I returned to my writing after class was over. Writing about the situation and describing what happened during the group sessions—the students' perspectives, my own thoughts, and the relation between these data sources—helped me locate and define the parameters of the problem. Second, I talked with my colleagues about my tension.

They offered ideas and new possibilities for me to consider, based on their experiences and ideas gleaned from research in teacher education.

Next I began to analyze why there were differences in perspectives. First, students felt that the guides took too much time to complete—time that they would rather have spent reading and thinking about the ideas. Because I had not tried the task of completing the readings and guides myself, I did not realize this problem. Second, students felt that the guides were like minitests, not tools to make sense of ideas. This perspective caused me to reconsider what questions I thought were helpful strategies to facilitate meaning and those that students interpreted as "test questions." Students understood my perspective regarding the need for them to grapple with ideas prior to class and come prepared to talk about issues. Some shared that they would rather write summaries of key points drawn from the articles or complete response activities that could then be used in later assignments, like a theoretical framework paper. Others noted that they would prefer to write their own notes or visual maps of ideas. They suggested that I could assess their understandings via their performances during discussions and examine their alternate tools for how well they had constructed meaning. The students helped me rethink the purpose of the reading guides from their perspectives as well as my own. The result was that the students helped me develop tools that were purposeful and meaningful to them and that supported their learning. My inquiry continued as I tried new ways to help students read and talk about course concepts, collected additional students' perspectives about the usefulness of new forms of response, and assessed the quality of students' weekly written work, daily discussions, and final projects.

Taking Inquiry One Step Further: Using a Critical Perspective

The example presented in the previous section shows how a tension can be formulated into an inquiry problem and data can be collected, described, analyzed, and interpreted. An additional step in the inquiry process is to critically examine issues under study, asking difficult questions about equity versus inequality and how practices in school reproduce or contest inequities. Other critical questions include examining the conditions in classrooms that empower some students and disempower others. The work of theorists like Michael Apple and Patrick Shannon help us think about schools as political places where teachers must ask questions about what they need to do to bring about societal change and how they can empower students to do the same. For example, Shannon (1990) discusses the concept of *critical literacy,* (not to be confused with critical thinking), which he defines as the process of reflecting on what we say and do to identify the social forces that influence our actions. Critical literacy also requires educators to take a moral and ethical stand for the beliefs and actions we adhere to.

Teachers who take this critical approach would examine their beliefs and actions and identify tensions in their teaching or classrooms. But these tensions might be generated as a result of looking closely at what we do and say during classroom interactions and asking questions about inequity and disempowering students. Educators taking a critical literacy stance would seek to understand the educational experiences of all students and study who learns in particular classrooms and how they learn. They would consistently pay attention to how some ways of knowing (or learning) and knowledge are valued or privileged over other ways. And teachers using a critical approach would study the contexts in which learning occurs within the classroom and beyond. For example, they would situate events and actions historically, culturally, and socially while thinking about issues of equity and social justice.

Reflection Point_____

Revisit your responses to previous Reflection Points in this chapter, particularly your description of a typical day in your classroom. Use a critical literacy stance to analyze events, actions, and interactions. Do you see inequity in the tasks or interactions that occur between peers and/or you and your students? Are some students empowered and others disempowered? Why might this occur? What new tensions emerge for you that could be formulated into inquiry problems?

Other Considerations Related to the Inquiry Process

It is very useful to sort out tensions, formulate inquiry problems, and attempt to solve them on your own. But there is also great value in working with trusted colleagues who are committed, as you are, to asking difficult questions that move us forward in our thinking and actions. To make change both within and beyond our classrooms—to affect students and schools districtwide—it is essential to collaborate with parents and other community members as we talk about and define inquiry problems. Once problems are defined, collaboratively crafting an inquiry plan to work on various dimensions of the problem is important. This ensures that many perspectives and stakeholders are represented in the planning, data collection, analysis, and interpretation phases of the inquiry project; it also improves the likelihood that findings will be deemed credible and useful.

Another consideration about teaching and learning tensions is that they usually are presented as dichotomies that force us to view issues as black or white when the tensions are typically multihued. As educators we are constantly choosing along a continuum of possible choices, matching our pedagogy to the specific needs of students on a year-by-year, day-to-day, or moment-by-moment basis. It is precisely this ever-changing set of circumstances and actions that precipitates tensions, which in reality are indicators of responsive, planful teachers in action.

In dealing with the tensions in our lives and designing inquiry projects to understand and resolve issues, it is important to know that there is a considerable body of information from both the research and practice literature that can inform our literacy practices (for example, basic principles that can cut across similar sites and students). In the next section of this chapter I will present research on best practices and standards associated with the teaching of reading and writing. But there are cautions to consider when reading this information. First, we teach a diversity of learners and we have learned that a "one size fits all" approach does not work. This diversity has implications for how we address the tensions that emerge in our teaching each day. For example, it is useful to draw insights from colleagues' plans as we construct our own plans and unique visions of literacy pedagogy. However, it is not useful to appropriate another individual's philosophy, beliefs, vision, or pre-existing plans in a lock-step fashion because we are each unique as teachers and we work with unique groups of students in unique contexts. Finally, it is important to remember that students face their own tensions and challenges each day. Some of these are related to, although different than, our own. The tensions of these researchers are about academic choices and challenges, social and political forces, and the plain biological reality that they are developing rapidly as human beings. Responsive educators also must keep this sense of dynamic developmental changes in learners in sight.

The Role of Standards in Developing Responsive, Planful Teaching

Developing the skills needed to learn about learners, the ability to document and reflect on students' actions and our own practices, and the knowledge of how to take what is learned and apply it to practice is not an easy task. Nor is this process the same for every teacher. But this knowledge base is necessary in light of today's pressures to adopt particular materials and methods or certain research findings as a quick fix to meeting all students' literacy needs. This knowledge is also key to earning state licensure and achieving National Board for Professional Teaching Standards (NBPTS) certification. For example, the NBPTS has created propositions that describe what teachers should know and be able to do to affect students' learning and achievement in positive ways. The five propositions that follow are research based, sound, and useful for literacy educators as they think about moral purpose, vision, tensions that emerge between beliefs and practices, and inquiry projects designed to address these tensions.

1. Teachers are committed to students and their learning.

2. Teachers know the subjects they teach and how to teach those subjects to students.

3. Teachers are responsible for managing and monitoring student learning.

4. Teachers think systematically about their practice and learn from experiences.

5. Teachers are members of learning communities.

(A complete list of the five propositions and definitions for each is provided in Appendix B on pages 161–164.)

Coupled with the NBPTS standards are propositions that focus on best practices for teaching and learning in general and reading and writing in particular. These are outlined in Zemelman, Daniels, and Hyde's (1998) book titled *Best Practice: Standards for Teaching and Learning in America's Schools.* The list of best practice associated with students' learning is included in Box 4-2. This list is a set of research-based, interlocking principles that characterizes how students learn and thus impacts the type of learning experiences that should occur across and between content areas and grade levels. The larger lists of best practices in reading and writing, including practices to increase or decrease, are provided in Appendix C on pages 165–167.

Literacy researchers have generated principles or best practices that focus specifically on the effective teaching of literacy. These include the following:

Standards for the English Language Arts (International Reading Association & National Council of Teachers of English, 1996)

10 Principles of Effective Teaching of Reading (Tompkins, 1997)

Learning to Read: Core Understandings (Braunger & Lewis, 1997)

These lists are provided in Appendixes D, E, and F respectively.

Reflection Point _____

Read the information that outlines each of the five NBPTS propositions and the best practice principles. Write a short description of what each of the five NBPTS propositions means to you. Describe what each best practice principle looks like "in action" in your classroom or professional practices.

Consider the list of recommendations for best practices in reading and writing (see Appendix C). What practices in the "increase category" do you currently see in your practices? What practices in the "decrease" category do you see in your practices?

What tensions emerge for you after examining the NBPTS propositions and the lists of best practices?

BOX 4-2
Principles of Best Practice for Learning

STUDENT-CENTERED: The best starting point for schooling is young people's real interests; all across the curriculum, investigating students' own questions should always take precedence over studying arbitrarily and distantly selected "content."

EXPERIENTIAL: Active, hands-on, concrete experience is the most powerful and natural form of learning. Students should be immersed in the most direct possible experience of the content of every subject.

HOLISTIC: Children learn best when they encounter whole ideas, events, and materials in purposeful contexts, not by studying subparts isolated from actual use.

AUTHENTIC: Real, rich, complex ideas and materials are at the heart of the curriculum. Lessons or textbooks that water-down, control, or oversimplify content ultimately disempower students.

EXPRESSIVE: To fully engage ideas, construct meaning, and remember information, students must regularly employ the whole range of communicative media—speech, writing, drawing, poetry, dance, drama, music, movement, and visual arts.

REFLECTIVE: Balancing the immersion in experience and expression must be opportunities for learners to reflect, debrief, abstract from their experiences what they have felt and thought and learned.

SOCIAL: Learning is always socially constructed and often interactional; teachers need to create classroom interactions that "scaffold" learning.

COLLABORATIVE: Cooperative learning activities tap the social power of learning better than competitive and individualistic approaches.

DEMOCRATIC: The classroom is a model community; students learn what they live as citizens of the school.

COGNITIVE: The most powerful learning comes when children develop true understanding of concepts through higher order thinking associated with various fields of inquiry and through self-monitoring of their thinking.

DEVELOPMENTAL: Children grow through a series of definable but not rigid stages, and schooling should fit its activities to the developmental level of students.

CONSTRUCTIVIST: Children do not just receive content; in a very real sense, they re-create and reinvent every cognitive system they encounter, including language, literacy, and mathematics.

CHALLENGING: Students learn best when faced with genuine challenges, choices, and responsibility in their own learning.

From Zemelman, S., Daniels, H. & Hyde, A. (1998). *Best practice: New standards for teaching and learning in America's schools* (2nd ed.). Portsmouth, NH: Heinemann.

A Caution About Best Practices and Standards

The best practices and standards provided here allow us to see what effective practices might look like in action in various teachers' classrooms. But the fact remains that standards will look different in each teacher's classroom because he or she has individual ways of interpreting the guidelines for the diversity of learners in a respective classroom, coupled with the developmental level of these students and what approaches best support their learning. That is why we have a set of "best practices" (plural) not *the* best way to achieve a set of goals.

Further, it is important to remember that standards and state proficiencies are created by individuals for a variety of reasons, not the least of which are political in nature. Standards have been developed to provide benchmarks to guide teachers' pedagogy, to hold educators accountable for students' learning, and to hold students' accountable. Standards can offer important goals for students' learning with the knowledge that how teachers and students attain these goals is negotiable based on students' interests and needs. But standards are equally dangerous when they become prescriptive and negate meaningful learning, or when they are used to judge teachers or students' efforts in unfair ways. They are dangerous when they contribute to inequities, disempowering students, and social injustice. We must constantly ask ourselves when standards or someone else's picture of best practices may be receiving too much of our attention to the detriment of individual learners in our classroom.

A Strategy for Thinking About Learners

Tensions and beliefs as well as standards and best practices are indeed powerful forces that shape the nature of teaching and learning in our classrooms. In addition, the ideas put forth by cultural theorists such as Heath, Au, and Moll (see Chapter 3) as well as the issues raised by critical theorists such as Shannon (this chapter) about what occurs within our classrooms that privileges some learners over others are also important factors to address. In this chapter we have focused on ourselves as learners and teachers as a strategy for gleaning insight into the way we view learning and teaching. In the next chapter we will return to a focus on students and what occurs during interactions in our classrooms on a daily basis.

Trevor Cairney offers a strategy that allows us to refocus on learners without negating the importance of teachers, interactions, or classroom contexts. In his book *Pathways to Literacy*, Cairney (1995) talks about the many challenges facing educators as they seek to renew their practice. He urges that as educators rethink their pedagogies, they resist the pressure to become caught up in debates over methods, materials, and procedures. Instead, Cairney believes that we should focus on three key issues to inform our pedagogy:

- peer and teacher-student interactions and the relationships that we permit and encourage in our classrooms

- the conditions that we set up in our classrooms that foster learning

- the interactions and discourses that we promote and the extent to which some students are empowered or disempowered by discourses we privilege

Using these three issues to focus our renewal, Cairney believes that we can work to meet all students' needs. We have explored several of these ideas already throughout previous chapters, and I will focus on these ideas throughout the remainder of the book. With this in mind, let's examine current research knowledge about learning, teaching, and literacy that we can use to inform our practice.

Chapter 5

Using Knowledge About Learners and Relationships, and Recognizing the Conditions That Foster Learning

1. *Are you a reader? YES. I LIKE TO READ R L STINE BOOK— THEY ARE SUSPENCE.*

2. *How do you know if someone is a good reader? IF THE READER IS FAIRLY QUICK.*

3. *How do you think that teachers decide who is a good reader? THEIR SPEED AND THEIR GRAMMOR.*

4. *If you had your choice, what type of books would you like to read for math class? NOVEL.*

5. *What advice would you give someone who wanted to get better at reading math? PAY ATTENTION IN CLASS.*

6. *If you had your choice what topic would you like for a story problem to cover? ICE SKATING.*

7. *What are your thoughts when you read a story problem? I SAY TO MYSELF "OH MAN A STORY PROBLEM. I HATE THESE THINGS."*

8. *How do you know what to do in a story problem? READ IT CAREFULLY.*

9. *When do you have to read math besides the times you read a story problem? A WORD EQUATION.*

10. *Is reading important in math class? Why or why not? YES BECAUSE THEY HAVE STORY PROBLEMS AND WORD EQUATIONS.*

11. *What are your strengths in working story problems? I HAVE*
    NONE. Your weaknesses? ALL OF IT—BASICALLY COM-
    PERINDING IT.

12. *What is most important to understand about working story*
    problems? READ IT CAREFULLY AND KNOW WHAT YOU
    ARE READING.

13. *Are you a writer? NO. What do you think makes a good writer?*
    SPELLING, GRAMMAR, PUNCTUATION, AND NOT HAV-
    ING RUN-ON SENTENCES.

14. *What kind of writing do you have to do in math class? GIVE*
    DIRECTIONS FOR MAPS.

15. *What kind of writing would you like to do in math class?*
    NONE. Is writing important in math class? NO BECAUSE
    YOU REALLY ONLY NEED NUMBERS.

> *Morrisa's written responses (in caps) from a questionnaire she*
> *filled out in her high school math class*

Gleaning Insight About Students as People

Responses like Morrisa's help us gain insight into students' perspectives about learning, literacy, and math, but teachers also see glimpses of who students are as people—their likes, dislikes, fears, and beliefs. Just as we need to understand ourselves as teachers and persons including our moral purposes, vision, tensions, literacy histories, and beliefs about teaching and learning—we need to learn about students as learners and people. This insight is very important in light of research in the field of education and literacy that suggests that such understanding about our students allows us to build relationships with them that are grounded on our knowledge about their home and school lives and their personal interests and goals. Because of this insight we can provide more meaningful learning opportunities for students (see Dillon, 1989; Dillon & Moje, 1998).

In Chapter 3 I discussed the work of Luis Moll who has conducted research on the power of teachers' learning about the cultural funds of knowledge students glean at home and in their communities—knowledge that we can build on in school. Likewise I shared Rick Umpleby's belief in learning about his students' home lives; this included Rick talking with parents and kids outside of school, and working with kids in extracurricular activities to interact with them in different contexts. However, co-researchers Fred Erickson and Jeffery Schultz (1992) have discovered that little research has focused on understanding students' lives in schools, particularly the interaction between their social, emotional, and cognitive experiences. Often, when students are studied in school settings, they are studied and characterized as a monolithic group (e.g., adolescents). A logical option is focusing on individual students and their unique characteristics (Dillon & Moje, 1998). Nevertheless, a concern associated with learning about individual students—above and beyond the logistics of finding the time to gather and analyze data—is, How can we use this information for the betterment of the whole class as well as the individual? Meeting this challenge seems possible at the elementary level but appears almost insurmountable at the secondary level. However, teachers like Joe Ruhl, Rick Umpleby, and Donna and Teresa, the two math teachers who designed the questionnaire that began this chapter, have taught me that it can be done.

Donna and Teresa are in the same math department at Jefferson High School and often team together to plan and work with students. During a Lafayette School Corporation (LSC) staff development program David O'Brien and I provided leadership for, they identified a goal of developing new pedagogies to meet the needs of their lowest achieving students. One idea they gleaned from their professional reading was the connection between literacy and math, and they set out to learn more about this as well as powerful literacy strategies they could offer students to help them understand difficult math concepts. Because these teachers had not immediately seen the connection between math and literacy, they wondered what their "at risk" learners thought about learning, mathematics, and literacy. Thus, as part of a professional development inquiry project, Donna and Teresa designed a questionnaire and administered it to their lowest achieving students. Together the two teachers analyzed the questionnaires by first looking at each student's comments and then looking across all students' comments for patterns of responses (see Box 5-1 for the questionnaire and strategies to analyze responses).

BOX 5-1
Donna and Teresa's Questionnaire and Analysis Strategies

1. Are you a reader? What do you like to read?
2. What do you like most about reading?
3. How do you know if someone is a good reader?
4. How do you think that teachers decide who is a good reader?
5. If you had your choice, what type of books would you like to read for math class?
6. What books or other things have you read that you'd recommend for use with math class?
7. What advice would you give someone who wanted to get better at reading math?
8. If you had your choice, what topic would you like for a story problem to cover?
9. What are your thoughts when you read a story problem?
10. When do you have to read math besides the times you read a story problem?
11. Is reading important in math class? Why or why not?
12. What are your strengths in working story problems? Your weaknesses?
13. What is most important to understand about working story problems?
14. What is the most difficult part of doing a story problem? The easiest part?
15. What you like most about math is.... What you like least is....
16. When you are doing a story problem you need the most help when you are....
17. When you get stuck on a story problem what do you do to get unstuck?
18. Are you a writer? What do you write?
19. What do you like most about writing?
20. What do you think makes a good writer?
21. How do you think your teachers decide who is a good writer?
22. What kind of writing do you have to do in math class?
23. What kind of writing would you like to do in math class?
24. Is writing important in math class?

Analysis Strategies

1. Donna and Teresa read through the questionnaires one by one. They took a close look at the compiled responses to questions on the survey such as, Are you a reader? What do you like to read? They looked for patterns of responses that characterized students' thoughts and listed these patterns as they read through the responses. They compared their results and talked about discrepancies. They generated a final list of patterns.

2. Donna and Teresa read through the surveys again, tallying the number of student responses that they categorized under each pattern previously generated. They generated frequency counts that gave them a broad sense of students' ideas.

3. Donna and Teresa divided the pile of responses in half and read through the surveys again, looking at each one as an individual case. They wrote brief statements summarizing what they learned about each individual and then shared their summaries with each other.

4. Donna and Teresa asked themselves, What do these findings tell us about individuals? About the group of students we work with in our math classes? How will these data inform our teaching and classroom practices?

Donna and Teresa were excited about what they learned from individual students and they constructed implications from the findings to inform their practice. They also were surprised at the insights they gleaned about students' interests, needs, fears, and strengths. They were interested in what the students had to say about literacy in math class because both teachers were committed to using reading, writing, and talk as ways for students to learn and demonstrate mathematical knowledge. As Donna noted,

> A great deal was learned from the survey. We understand much more about the students and we plan to share this information with the kids' English teachers, too. For, example, our students detest writing in math. They tell us "This isn't English class—we shouldn't have to write in math class." But we have to help our students learn a better way to explain the math they use to solve problems. I have designed a two-column method that I am testing right now where they do the mathematics on one side of the paper and explain each step completed on the other side. I am also interested in adding daily journal writing to the class. I will give students prompts to get at their feelings about the lessons, opportunities to ask questions, explanations of concepts and processes.

When data from students are used to improve their learning, students recognize this. The fact that educators value students' input serves to build strong relationships between students and their teachers.

Like Donna and Teresa, teachers from other disciplines who participated in the LSC professional development program gathered data about students' interests, perceptions, and needs to complement other assessment data they collected (e.g., assignments, test scores). Sometimes methods of gleaning students' perspectives were informal and quick, which allowed the teacher to use on-the-spot information to affect relationship building and learning. For example, on the first day of class every semester Joe Ruhl asks his students to pair up and interview each other to "find out something interesting about your partner." Students find out about peers' hobbies, interests in and out of school, and jobs. I watched Joe initiate this activity by explaining, "it's just like Mr. Rogers says on TV—you're special, there's nobody like you—just like genetics." Each partner stands and introduces the other, sharing what they've learned (with the interviewee politely correcting information as needed). Joe always adds a comment or asks a question after each presentation as a way of connecting with the interviewee. For example, Jackie, a student in Joe's biology class, introduced her partner Jennifer and related that Jennifer works part time after school at a fast-food restaurant. Joe smiled and said, "Jennifer, now I know which restaurant to go to and I will be sure to give you a hard time when I place my order! Just kidding." Jennifer beamed with pleasure and a bit of embarrassment. In that moment Joe connected with her, as a person. Tina, another student in the class, commented after several weeks of school, "Mr. Ruhl even knows my name and he cares about whether I learn." The introductory activity Joe used also served the purpose of community building—helping students in the class get to know one another as individuals, not just fellow students. Many of these students know little about the lives of their peers except maybe their school cliques; in Joe's class they not only heard about a diversity of their peers' activities, but they also observed a teacher validating students' interests and connecting life in and outside of school.

Powerful teaching occurs when teachers make connections with students as people *and* as learners. Rick Umpleby stressed that we must "show them that we care about them and want them to learn." In previous chapters of this book I defined responsive, planful teaching. The teachers I have introduced throughout the book serve as models of many key concepts that underlie this thinking about teaching and learning. As discussed in Chapter 2, responsive teachers engage in reflection, inquiry, and knowledge-building activities. And in Chapter 4 I noted that teachers who examine their beliefs and practices and analyze the tensions they encounter in their daily teaching often determine areas in which they need new knowledge to meet the needs of all learners. In the next section I will present an overview of current research on how students learn and our role as teachers in this process. This knowledge base is the foundation for the conditions needed in our classrooms and schools to support all students' learning. Before we move on, take some time to address the questions in the following Reflection Point.

Reflection Point

Develop a short five-question interview guide (create a sheet with space for written responses between each question). This guide will allow you to gather data about each of your students. Craft questions that allow you to learn about students as individuals as well as learners.

Design an activity in class in which you can collect the interview data or pull students aside during individual work time or over the lunch hour.

Audiotape your conversations. Taping allows you to focus on the speaker and you can listen to the tape multiple times to review key points. You also can hear the expression in the speaker's voice—a key to understanding the message in a richer way. An advantage to writing short answers on an interview guide as you ask students the questions is that the data are then partially transcribed and you can look at them when comparing responses across students.

Analyze the responses. What do you learn about individuals? How might you use these insights to impact learning experiences and your pedagogy?

How Do Students Learn and What Is Our Role as Responsive Educators?

> I dislike school because it's too long and I hate scolding speeches. I really hate lectures—anything that has to do with sitting there and watching a teacher—I tend to doze off. I like hands on—you get to feel what it's like.
>
> Carolyn, interview from biology class

In the next section I will continue to discuss responsive teaching and the beliefs about learning and literacy espoused and enacted by responsive teachers. First, I will compare the concept of responsive, planful teaching to a *student-centered approach* to teaching. These perspectives share some common characteristics but differ in some ways. For example, teachers who embrace a student-centered approach focus on students' interests and learning needs. However, recently educators have cautioned that this perspective may imply that the teacher's content and learning goals are not important. Responsive educators believe that both teachers and students have important social and academic agendas that must be considered during interactions and literacy lessons. In addition, responsive teachers are knowledgeable about the concepts students need to learn and the strategies that are helpful to their learning. But these teachers take their cues on when to introduce new concepts and how to teach students (particular activities and approaches) from the interests and learning needs of individuals in their classrooms. For example, when Joe Ruhl moved to a mastery learning approach, with cooperative groups working on study guides and multiple labs to learn biology, he quickly recognized that he was not going to be able to cover all the chapters in the textbook. Instead, he identified what he referred to as "pillars" of biology, and he focused his attention on helping students learn a few key ideas well, rather than a lot of ideas in a superficial manner.

Likewise, after analyzing videotape and audiotape data (e.g., the transcript of the group session in which students completed the study guide on the sheep liver fluke), Joe reconsidered how to best mesh his own agenda with students' agenda for school (e.g., having fun and learning with others). The results of our analysis with Joe are in Table 1 on page 106.

Responsive teaching is undergirded by several theories related to how individuals learn. The first theory is a *constructivist perspective of learning*. This perspective suggests that learning is a cognitive activity, that learners actively construct their own understandings as they engage in reading and writing activities, and that learners use their schema (mental structures and knowledge) as they construct new ideas linking the new to their prior knowledge and experiences. As Au (1998) notes, constructivist approaches to literacy are characterized by lessons in which teachers involve students in reading and writing tasks and teach skills within meaningful literacy activities. Au lists several examples of constructivist approaches

Table 1
Merging Student and Teacher Agendas: Our Analysis

WHAT WE LEARNED ABOUT TEACHING AND LEARNING	SOURCES OF LEARNING	HOW WHAT WE'VE LEARNED WILL AFFECT FUTURE TEACHING AND LEARNING:

• Students want to be recognized and treated as persons; need individualized attention—to know that teachers care about them.	• Structured interviews with students
	  - Joe's beliefs
	  - Observation
	• Watching videotapes
	• Conversations with Deb and Dave
		• Continue to spend in/out of class time building relationships with students.
		• Continue to spend time constructing a risk-free environment in the classroom.
		• Monitor students' affective development along with their cognitive development.

• Students have their own agendas for school/specific classes; they must be persuaded to "buy" the product—biology.	• Watching videotapes • Conversations with Deb and Dave • Reading and reflecting on field notes and lesson transcripts	• Recognize students' agendas for school and learning; work to adapt teacher and student agendas so common ground is reached. • Observe students' actions and consider broader issues.
• Students want/need to have fun during the process of learning; they appreciate and respond positively to humor from their teacher.	• Structured interviews with students • Observations, field notes • Reading and reflecting on lesson transcripts	• Continue to make learning fun by interspersing humor into content learning activities; take risks as a teacher by being unpredictable and an entertainer at times; allow student humor. • Consider whether the assigned tasks are interesting and fun; can the tasks be completed in a fun way?
• Students need to be active learners—to move around the room, participate in several different types of activities within one class period, to individually manipulate materials even when working collectively on group tasks.	• Joe's beliefs • Observations • Watching videotapes • Structured interviews with students	• Continue to allow and provide opportunities for student movement in the classroom • Structure individual lessons so they include several activities ranging from whole-class to small-group to partners to individual work. • Observe small-group work to see who manipulates materials; provide opportunities for all students to become actively involved in lessons.

continued

Table 1
Merging Student and Teacher Agendas: Our Analysis (continued)

• Students do not like anything that slightly resembles a lecture (whole-class activities) even if the presentation provides active student involvement or multimedia presentations; students can't discriminate effective lectures/presentations from ineffective ones.	• Structured interviews with students • Joe's beliefs • Observations • Watching videotapes • Reflecting on lesson transcripts • Conversations with Deb and Dave	• Reflect on what works/doesn't during lecture presentations • Realize that many students can't distinguish/appreciate well-prepared teacher presentations/lectures because their need for social agendas can't be met as in small-group work.
• Students recognize the purposes for, and rationale behind the Mastery Learning approach; they appreciate the opportunity for a second chance to learn and earn a higher grade.	• Structured interviews with students • Observations • Informal conversations with students during class	• Continue to use Mastery Learning approach despite colleague/peer pressure to discontinue this approach. • Observe and question how students interpret/use mastery learning; monitor each step of the process for possible adaptation/improvement.
• Students see practice activities, to be completed in preparation for test B, as helpful—not as punishment. They do not believe they are viewed as dumb by those students who pass Test A.	• Field notes • Conversations with Deb and Dave • Structured interviews with students • Observations	• Observe students who do practice activities versus students who do enrichment activities for affective differences between these groups. • Examine and revise practice activities. • Allow students who finish practice activities to do enrichment activities if they so desire. • Monitor teacher-student interactions as students complete practice activities.
• Students like group work, but self-selected groups only; when asked to reflect on their favorite activity/memory of biology they mentioned the fun they had working in groups and believed they learned better in small groups.	• Observations • Structured interviews with students • Field notes and videotapes • Conversations with Deb and Dave	• Allow students to self-select their groups. • Honor requests from students to switch groups. • Monitor small-group activities to understand further how students construct meaning together. • Help students learn to work cooperatively. • Continue to study the social and academic agendas of students and how these interact during small-group work. • Examine student roles during group work and and how these roles are related to learning.

continued

Table 1
Merging Student and Teacher Agendas: Our Analysis (continued)

• Students found labs and simulation games fun and useful for learning/ reinforcing biology concepts; they found these activities useful for learning how to do science.	• Structured interviews with students • Observations, video-tapes, field notes • Lesson transcripts	• Continue spending class time doing lab work and simulations. • Continue to restructure lab guides • Observe students as they do labs to determine what tasks/roles students assign themselves/ each other and why.
• Students tend to focus on task completion as opposed to the process of understanding biology concepts.	• Observations, videotapes • Field notes, lesson transcripts, reflecting on transcripts • Conversation with Deb and Dave • Structured interviews with students	• In revising study guides and labs, continue to set up road blocks that focus students on the process of doing biology and understanding biology concepts. • In working with students one-to-one in small groups, be aware of their goal of getting answers (product) from the teacher—set up verbal "roadblocks" and activities that make students accountable for process.

including process writing, literature-based instruction, and balanced literacy instruction.

As noted earlier, however, learning is more than just a cognitive process. It is also a *social process* (see Dixon-Krauss, 1996; Vygotsky, 1978) in which individuals construct meaning through their interactions with other people and the environment. Vygotsky promoted a *sociocultural perspective* about how students learn (Cairney, 1995). This perspective helps us understand that literacy learning is embedded in culture—the beliefs, values, ideas, and knowledge shared by a group of people—and conversely contributes to the shaping of culture. Students construct meaning on a daily basis and this meaning-construction process is influenced by the cultural backgrounds, practices, and knowledge students bring to learning situations and those they create as a result of taking part in a classroom or activity. This includes the funds of knowledge or cultural capital learners bring from home to school (Moll, 1992), the student's learning experiences over time, and the student's experiences with others on a daily basis in and out of school. (See Box 5-2 for considerations about the social constructiveness of literacy.)

> **BOX 5-2**
> **Important Considerations About the**
> **Social Constructiveness of Literacy**
>
> - Readers and writers create meaning; they don't simply transcribe, summarize or extract it.
> - The meaning readers and writers create is always greater than the written text's potential meaning and the literacy user's prior knowledge and experiences.
> - No two readers or writers can ever read or write the same text in the same way; nor do they arrive at the same meaning as part of these processes.
> - Above all, meaning is relative, socially constructed, and only relevant within the context of the social purposes and relationships to which the reading or writing is directed.
>
> From Cairney, T.H. (1995). *Pathways to literacy*. London: Cassell.

Within a social interactionist perspective is the research on *scaffolded instruction* or what Wood, Bruner, and Ross (1976) refer to as the role of tutoring in problem solving. Scaffolded instruction is grounded in the belief that a supportive or more knowledgeable person (peer or teacher) can help a student moves from one level of learning to a higher one as the child increases his or her mastery of a given task. However as Meyer (1993) notes, how this support "is built, maintained, and then gradually withdrawn is more complex that the simple metaphor implies" (p. 41). Linked with scaffolded instruction is the concept of the Zone of Proximal Development (ZPD) (Vygotsky, 1978), or the distance between the actual developmental level of a child and the level of his or her potential development with the guidance of a more capable peer or a teacher. Learning generally occurs when students are supported by teachers as they take risks and explore new ideas within this zone. This is a useful way to think about learning and our role as the teacher in this process. Rogoff (1990) adds the concept of *guided participation* to Vygotsky's ZPD because she believes that students and others collaborate to build bridges, connecting students' current knowledge and skills to new knowledge and skills. This collaborative process involves intersubjectivity or the sharing of focus and purpose between a student and a more knowledgeable other. This collaboration is a cognitive as well as a social and emotional exchange between teachers and students.

Responsive, planful educators recognize the importance of the re-search on child-centered approaches, schema theory and constructivist perspectives, social interactionist and sociocultural perspectives, and the role of scaffolding and the ZPD. Responsive teachers do not view learning as a step-by-step or linear process, nor as movement through stages. Rather, they believe that *teachers and students learn in tandem, moment-by-moment.* Thus, responsive teachers draw from literacy theory and content knowledge, knowledge about learners, and knowledge about particular students' cognitive and affective strengths and needs as they make on-going pedagogical decisions. These decisions also are shaped by what is needed on certain tasks, at certain times, by particular learners, and in particular situations or learning contexts.

The Affective Dimensions of Learning

> I like Mr. Ruhl's class—it is fun and interesting. He makes us do our labs and everything right. We work in study groups and we can have four different conversations going on and still get it [work] done. It's weird you know, you can be sitting there talking about schoolwork and about answers to one question and then we flip off the subject and go to an-other one...and then flip back and we get it [the study guide] answered.
> Carolyn, interview from biology class

Students' affective and emotional perspectives about learning, as in-dicated in Carolyn's comments, also influence how they construct mean-ing and how they act and interact during classroom lessons. Recent literacy research has focused on students' motivation to learn and their engagement in various activities. As noted by prominent researchers in the area of reading engagement (see Guthrie & Wigfield, 1997) an en-gagement perspective takes into account both the cognitive and motiva-tional aspects of literacy and provides a more complete description of how students read and become involved in literacy activities.

Motivation theorists such as Pintrich and Schunk (1996) propose that an individual's beliefs, values, and goals for achievement are critical in-fluences in their achievement-related behavior. Building on these ideas Wigfield (1997) presents the following constructs as questions; these con-structs relate to motivation in general and literacy in particular.

- Can I succeed? Can I be a good reader?

- Do I want to succeed and why? Do I want to be a good reader and why?

- What do I need to do to succeed? What do I need to do to be a good reader?

To answer the question, Can I be a good reader?, assumes that students can assess their *ability beliefs* or evaluate their competence in various areas. For example, if students believe they have the ability to accomplish a task (e.g., read a particular book), then this often relates to and predicts their success with this task. Students' *expectancy* or sense of how well they will do on a task (versus how good they are at a task) also predicts their success (e.g., I know I will be able to understand the ideas in this biology chapter on cells). Last, students' *self-efficacy*—the beliefs a person has about his or her capabilities to learn or perform behaviors at designated levels (Bandura, 1986)—is a major determinate when choosing activities or being willing to expend effort and being persistent in completing tasks (e.g., I know I have the ability to get an "A" on this test if I complete the study guide and study at home). Research indicates that with multiple experiences, students can develop self-efficacy. When students believe they are competent readers and writers, they will be more likely to engage in reading and writing activities.

If we hope to motivate students, then they must answer the question, Do I want to be a good reader?, with an affirmative "yes." This is an important question when we consider the research that indicates that some students are able to read but have no desire to do so. Desiring to be a good reader is based on the *subjective task value* or a student's incentive for engaging in an activity. The value of a task includes the student's interest in the task, whether he or she believes the task is important, and whether the task is deemed useful. Research indicates that students' subjective task value predicts their intentions and the decisions they make to continue reading and writing. Another construct related to the question, Do I want to be a good reader?, is *intrinsic motivation*, which involves completing a task because you are interested in the task. Another factor is *extrinsic motivation*, or being motivated to complete a task by external reasons like prizes or being told to complete the task by a teacher. The second part of the question, Why do I want to be a good reader?, relates to two other constructs, the first of which is *achievement goals* or the purposes students have for reading. This includes the goal to learn an activity and the desire to outperform others. The second construct, *subjective values*, was discussed previously and includes interest, attainment, and utility associated with tasks.

Answers to the question, What do I need to do to be a good reader?, are grounded in the constructs of *strategy use*, or whether students believe strategies are helpful to their learning; *volition*, or the voluntary sustained effort to complete tasks despite distractions; *self-regulation*, or setting goals to gauge one's progress, self-evaluating to compare present performance with goals, and self-reactions; and *help seeking*. There is evidence that suggests that these constructs connect cognition and motivation (Wigfield, 1997). (See Box 5-3 for more resources on motivation and reading engagement.)

Learners' beliefs, self-efficacy, expectation that they will do well, interest in tasks, involvement, and use of strategies to help themselves succeed play a crucial role in their individual motivation to achieve. We do know that motivated learners are usually *engaged learners*, and developing this type of learner is our goal as educators. The theories and concepts about learning and learners outlined previously provide an important backdrop for our continued conversation about developing pedagogies that support students' learning.

BOX 5-3
Resources to Learn More About
Motivation and Reading Engagement

Gambrell, L.B., Palmer, B.M., Codling, R.M., & Mazzoni, S.A. (1996). Assessing motivation to read. *The Reading Teacher, 49*, 518–533. (An instrument to measure two components of motivation in grades 2–6: self-concept and task value.)

Guthrie, J.T., & Wigfield, A. (Eds.). (1997). *Reading engagement: Motivating readers through integrated instruction*. Newark, DE: International Reading Association.

Henk, W.A., & Melnick, S.A. (1995). The Reader Self Perception Scale (RSPS): A new tool for measuring how children feel about themselves as readers. *The Reading Teacher, 48*, 470–482. (This self-assessment scale measures the way learners appraise themselves as readers.)

Pintrich, P.R., & Schunk, D.H. (1996). *Motivation in education: Theory, research, and applications*. Englewood Cliffs, NJ: Merrill.

*Reflection Point*_____

What activities and contexts seem to help you become an engaged learner? Think about your own learning patterns and what motivates you.

Observe a literacy lesson in a colleague's classroom or watch a videotaped lesson from your own classroom. Watch for signs of engagement and disengagement on the same task. Try to determine why some students are engaged and others are not. Talk with your students; ask them what you could do to make the activity more interesting. Use their ideas and your own to think about adjustments that could be made to create a motivating activity or context for learning. Try the revised activity and document what happens.

Conditions That Support Learning and Learners

The ideas about motivation and engagement presented in this chapter provide a compelling case as we think about the ways we set up our classrooms, design classroom experiences, and the pedagogies we use to support students' learning. For example, Cairney (1995) notes that students learn best in an environment where they see purposes for learning and can connect these to their lives in and out of school, when they engage in social relationships and groups, when they communicate ideas to others, and when they experience success.

Using 20 years of inquiry to guide his thinking, Brian Cambourne (1995) generated a set of conditions that he deems necessary to support and promote literacy learning:

- *Immersion*—Learners need to be immersed in text of all kinds.
- *Demonstration*—Learners need to receive many demonstrations of how texts are constructed and used.
- *Expectations*—Expectations of those to whom learners are bonded are powerful coercers of learners' behavior. "We achieve what we expect to achieve; we fail if we expect to fail; we are more likely to engage with demonstrations of those whom we regard as significant and who hold high expectations for us."

- *Responsibility*—Learners need to make decisions about when, how, and what "bits" to learn in any learning task. Learners who lose the ability to make decisions are disempowered.

- *Employment*—Learners need time and opportunity to use, employ, and practise their developing control in functional, realistic, and nonartificial ways.

- *Approximations*—Learners must be free to approximate the desired model—"mistakes" are essential for learning to occur.

- *Response*—Learners must receive feedback from exchanges with more knowledgeable others. Responses must be relevant, appropriate, timely, readily available, and nonthreatening, with no strings attached. (p. 187)

Engagement is the goal of employing these various conditions in the classroom. As Cambourne notes, engagement occurs when learners are convinced that

> they are potential doers or performers of these demonstrations they are observing. Engaging with these demonstrations will further the purposes of their lives. They can engage and try to emulate without fear of physical or psychological hurt if their attempts are not fully correct. Helping learners make these decisions constitutes the artistic dimensions of teaching. (1995, p. 187)

Other researchers also have documented actions of teachers who foster motivation in their classrooms. Turner and Paris (1995) conducted research to understand how classroom tasks affect students' motivation for literacy—their desire to read and write, their understanding of the goals of literacy, and the self-regulation processes of readers and writers. These researchers found that the most reliable indicator of motivation is not the type of reading program, but the daily tasks that teachers provide for students during classroom lessons. The tasks that are most successful in motivating students include (a) providing opportunities for students to use reading and writing for authentic purposes (like reading trade books and composing), (b) conveying the value of literacy for communication and enjoyment, and (c) allowing students to be actively involved in constructing meanings and metacognitions about literacy.

Turner and Paris also identified classroom lessons as open or closed. *Open tasks* are those in which students are in control of both the products they create and the processes they employ. There is no one answer or specified procedure to use. Open tasks are those that require students to set goals, select and organize information, choose strategies, and assess final results. *Closed tasks* are those in which the product, the process, or both are specified. These tasks afford students fewer opportunities to control their learning and explore their interests because these tasks do not permit students to make choices and decisions.

Finally, Turner and Paris offer six "C's" (see Box 5-4 on page 116), or ways teachers can foster motivation in their classrooms by changing the activities they ask students to engage in. These activities fit well with Cambourne's conditions of literacy learning.

Teachers who seek to meet the needs of all students in their classrooms draw from the conditions for learning outlined by Cambourne and Turner and Paris. But teachers do so in unique ways, matching or adapting strategies to students' needs and the content of the lesson. What follows is a transcript of a videotaped lesson from Rick Umpleby's classroom. First, I present the transcript in three parts, with an analysis of what happened following each respective segment. At the end of the last transcript segment, I present several of the conditions for learning that were evident during this lesson. I do want to note that all the conditions were evident at one time or another in Rick's room based on my analysis of lessons over time. In this transcript you will see the following conditions of learning:

- the concept of immersion with the use of multiple texts and a variety of activities;
- demonstrations of how to read and think about texts;
- high expectations or the belief that everyone can learn and engage in productive, meaningful work;
- responsibility for ones' own learning and that of others;
- employment of literacy skills and strategies presented in class and based on home and community knowledges;
- approximations that students felt free to make because of a risk-free environment; and

BOX 5-4
Turner and Paris's Six "C's"

Teachers who foster motivation in literacy classroom do so using the six "C's":

CHOICE: Provide students with authentic choices and purposes for literacy. These teachers recast activities to emphasize the enjoyment and informational value of literacy; do not refer to daily tasks as work but instead rename them by their function (e.g., ask students to plan an event by writing...and reading...).

CHALLENGE: Allow students to modify tasks so the difficulty and interest levels are challenging. These teachers demonstrate the many ways one can complete a task; show concrete examples to students of successful but different approaches to tasks; teach students to assess whether tasks are too difficult or too easy for them and how to adjust goals or strategies for appropriate difficulty; point out how students have molded tasks to their interests; and assign tasks that can be modified in many ways.

CONTROL: Show students how they can control their learning. These teachers teach students how to evaluate what they know and how to evaluate and monitor their learning. Students are probed by teachers with, Are you focused? What's more important? Students are guided to use inner speech so they can self-monitor.

COLLABORATION: Emphasize the positive aspects of giving and seeking help. These teachers provide students with opportunities to work with many different peers; students are taught how to teach each other by emphasizing the giving of clues not answers; many individual tasks are recast as paired or group tasks (e.g., paired reading vs. oral round-robin reading).

CONSTRUCTING MEANING: Emphasize strategies and metacognition for constructing meaning. These teachers realize that students need a repertoire of strategies in order to respond flexibly in reading and writing situations; students need extensive applications of comprehension as well as encoding and decoding strategies to assist them in acquiring an understanding of what literacy is as well as how to use and understand it.

CONSEQUENCES: Use the consequences of tasks to build responsibility, ownership, and self-regulation. These teachers acknowledge that group evaluation is a regular part of literacy instruction; students are encouraged to share their successes and failures; teachers help students to see that errorless learning is not learning at all, rather, real learning comes through error as errors provide information about needed improvement; teachers emphasize the value of effort and honing strategies because these tools equip students to attempt more and more challenging tasks. (1995, p. 672)

• responses by the teacher that affirmed students' responses or shifted them in new, more productive directions.

Using Conditions for Learning to Support All Students

Before class Rick stood at the opening of his classroom door and said something to every student who entered the classroom—a comment about the way they played in the basketball game the night before, how they looked or were dressed, a teasing or joking interchange—something that connected with each student on a personal level.

Umpleby: (teasing Bernard) Did you know Bernard was in the third quarter and fouled out [in the basketball game] last night? 'Course he wasn't alone. Six out of the first six that played fouled out so he had a lot of company! (Bernard smiles broadly and then sits down. The bell rings.)

Umpleby: OK, time to get started. (The students settle down for the most part and look up at Rick; he walks behind his lectern—a signal that he's ready to start class—and leans against it with his feet crossed. He begins to read aloud from the book *Edgar Allen*, a story about a Black child placed in a White foster family). When we left Edgar Allen last time it was shortly after the time when he had been given away [taken away from his foster family and placed with a "permanent" family] and the [foster] family was recovering and was making some progress toward getting back on track.... There's an episode today coming up though with the family...(he begins to read aloud from page 89 then stops at the bottom). Now, who's the one that seemed the most to want to keep him [Edgar]?

(Several students call out answers at the same time.)

Umpleby: Besides the two little ones [kids]...

Students: The mother.

Umpleby: The mother—she's the one that seems to be affected most by his departure. (He continues reading, stopping at places he's marked in his text ahead of time.)

Umpleby: The little kids believe that Edgar found his real parents as opposed to being given to strangers and Ryder [a newspaper reporter who visits the family] leaks the truth...all the sudden Ryder said, "Well, how do you feel about givin' him away?" Well the older folks [parents] know that they just gave him back [to the agency] so Ryder just let the cat out of the bag! Has Ryder messed things up?

Students: Yep, uh-huh.

Umpleby: Now the two little kids know. Well some folks just think they're smart and some folks think they're snoopy. Why Ryder is asking a 3- and 5-year-old this kind of stuff—well it's not real smart of him. Well the worst thing has happened hasn't it? The kids found out what the truth was and they're too young to understand the whole situation. Are they old enough to understand prejudice or hatred or race problems?

Students: Yeah...No...I think that the little girl will think she's next....

(Many students call out their ideas, some about the little kids thinking that they could be given away, too.)

Umpleby: Yes, why not? When you're little you don't know what the odds are that maybe somebody won't give you away, too. So when we pick it up again [the book] we'll see whether somebody can explain it [the situation] to the kids in reasonable terms, 'cause so far it doesn't look like it.

Analysis. Let's stop here and analyze what has happened so far. We see a classroom that is organized and arranged to support students' cognitive and affective learning. The interactions between Rick and the students also indicate mutual respect, active learning, and a sense of fun. Rick spent a lot of time engaged in relationship building at the beginning and end of class each day. Each day he stood at the doorway, welcoming and talking with students as they arrived for class. He also was able to monitor the hallway, urge or cajole kids to get to class on time, and touch base with his colleagues. As students entered the classroom, they talked to one another until the bell rang; they also could sit wherever they chose as long as they were quiet and attentive when class began. Rick's room was arranged with half the desks on one side, half on the other with all desks facing the middle of the room to encourage students to talk to one another, not to just address questions or responses to the teacher. Before and during class, Rick walked down the broad aisle in the middle of the room or stood at the opening of the desks at the front of the room.

Rick read aloud to his students every class period for at least 10 minutes. The current book, *Edgar Allen,* was chosen because Rick knew it would be of interest topically and emotionally to his students (several young women already had children of their own). He also knew the book provided opportunities to teach students important literacy knowledge. For example, as he read he stopped and discussed vocabulary words that he thought students might need help with or character motives and story events that led to future events. He also provided opportunities for students to connect many details together in the story or modeled how readers use details to foreshadow what might happen next in a story. As he read he involved students personally in the story by asking them to respond to the text in a variety of ways. Finally, he stopped to model what language sounds like or just to have fun with a segment of text.

As Rick's lesson continued, the class shifted to reading *The Old Man and the Sea* (1952), a book typically not used in low-track classrooms because it is considered too difficult for these students. Rick believed that this book, as well as others reserved for upper track students, had important ideas and themes that he wanted all students to explore. Thus, he developed a responsive teaching approach in which he supported the reading processes of his low-track students' and helped them understand the text. He also continually adapted his pedagogy to their needs. This approach to teaching included reading aloud portions of the book to the class as they read along silently, asking volunteers to help him by reading aloud short segments of the book, and having students read sections of the text aloud or silently in pairs and by themselves.

> **Umpleby:** OK, let's pass out the *Old Man* books. We'll see an attack here and there today and how the old man is faring. I hope the books last 'cause some of them are in sorry shape (teasing the students). (Students laugh and talk as they pass out books. Someone yells out that the pages of the book are falling out.)

> **Umpleby:** We finished yesterday with the line on page 100 that said, "It was an hour before the first shark hit him." Now they're [sic—the author] gonna describe that big shark that's coming up on the old man now. The paragraph

should start "The shark was not an accident." What do you remember from yesterday's reading that would have brought the shark?

Students: (many calling out the answer simultaneously) Uh, blood....

Umpleby: Blood from his harpoon. Now the old man's gonna be pretty quick here—he's pretty strong even though he's still tired and he's got some problems. It's what happens after this—his first attack—that's gonna get him in trouble. Now don't forget one thing—to fight these sharks we figured out, what did he have?

Students: A harpoon?

Umpleby: A harpoon. And what do you use with your hands?

Students: A knife?

Umpleby: And a club. And there's this little gaff—it is maybe only about this long (he shows them the length with his hands) and you use it to reach over and hook the fish and bring him in (Rick acts this out). He's not going to reach over to a shark with something that is that long. He'd lose his hand and the knife.

Yvonne: and the food he was bringing.

Umpleby: Yep, that's right. Oh, what about the old man's condition—besides being tired and hungry and worn out?

Students: His hands.

Umpleby: His hands—yeah, he's got some bad cuts across the top of his hands (Rick shows them with his hands) so to use these things against a big fish like the shark will probably be—he's gonna have to suffer some pain.

Later in the lesson dialogue continues.

Umpleby: The old man hits the shark between the two eyes...but there's a problem. Any of you killed a chicken? (Rick knew that several kids had because this was a major form of livelihood in the area.)

Students: Yeah.

Umpleby: Have you watched its nervous system—what happens?

Students: They shake—they keep on shaking.

Umpleby: Yeah, they shake and move a little bit. Some animals have a nervous system and I guess they don't die right away—

they keep on flipping. That shark will do something to hurt the old man (he reads on).

Umpleby: Well what snapped?

Yvonne: The rope?

Umpleby: Attached to what?

**Yvonne
and others:** The boat...the marlin...the fish the old man had.

Umpleby: What'd he kill him [shark] with?

Students: The harpoon!

This joint retelling of the story continued until they had reviewed the details of this event between the old man and the shark.

Umpleby: Now that's a heck of a shark and there will be others—others, what?

Students: Sharks!

Rick and the students continue reading, including a discussion of a religious reference/symbolism in the story. The students moan in disappointment when Rick says that they have to quit reading the day.

Analysis. The discussion of *The Old Man and the Sea* is an example of how Rick built on the language patterns of his predominately African American class of low-track readers and writers, adapting his discussion of class readings to this style of calling out answers and playful language and gesture described by Piestrup (1973) as "Black Artful." Students are active, motivated learners, constructing knowledge through interacting in an appropriate social, cultural context.

Rick's expertise lay in the balance between honoring students' cultural funds, yet empowering them to achieve academic and personal goals. For example, he knew that if students were to successfully understand *The Old Man and the Sea*, then he must scaffold their learning yet be responsive to their moment-by-moment needs. He accomplished this goal by helping learners *see* the story—he acted out segments using multiple voices and his hands to help students visualize vocabulary and events. Students also were encouraged to show their understanding of the story and themes derived from the text using multiple forms of representation.

In the last 10-minute excerpt from this lesson we see Rick focus students' attention on skill work. This activity appears to be one in which students are being asked to complete a traditional skills worksheet. But actually the sheet is being used because it provides information and a format that models the Basic Skills Test that students must pass to obtain a high school diploma.

Umpleby: OK, you may work in small groups or teams on the next task or you don't have to. (He passes out a worksheet for them to complete that covers skills on the BST. He explains the purpose of the assignment and says that they will do number one together.)

Umpleby: Yes, it's about misspellings, good. Can you guess how many words are wrong?

Students: 3? 6?

Umpleby: Six. Why 6?

Students: It [the sheet] tells ya.

Umpleby: All right! Let's go through number 1—give you an idea of what to do. What's the first thing you find? (students share responses) Nope. Business is right. (students call out other answers) Yeah, good. Why Brown's? What's in the word? (Students say "apostrophe.") Yeah, the apostrophe. There's no possession there. We're just talking about two people there—the Browns—so you take the apostrophe out. OK, one more. Marty, what do you think?

Marty: *There* (incorrect usage).

Umpleby: Yeah, what does *there* mean?

Marty: There—over yonder.

Umpleby: Yes, like "go there." OK. Let's work. It's up to you how you do the work—the duties of the team—but you need to turn in separate papers. (He circulates around the room, stopping to bend down and help students.)

The interactions in the three lesson segments presented in this section may look like many classroom sessions you have read about or participated in, but let's look below the surface to the "hidden curriculum." Take a moment now and look back at the introduction to this transcript where I noted the specific conditions for learning that would be evident in this lesson. Using this as a backdrop, let me analyze Rick's actions in more detail. First, Rick set up a safe and risk-free environment in his classroom where students felt good about their themselves as learners. Rick had *high expectations* of the learners in his classroom and because he believed in them and provided support for them to succeed, the students became partners in the learning process, attending class and actively participating in lessons. Students held Rick in high regard as a teacher (he had a very positive reputation as a caring educator who expected students to work but supported them in the process) and as a person (he was known to be funny and talk with his students before and after class). This mutual respect between the teacher and students was a key to meaningful learning in this classroom.

Rick employed a *predictable routine* in each class period. He read aloud to students, they worked as a whole class reading a book or writing on a topic, and students worked in small groups with Rick moving around to answer questions and observe actions. On occasion, students worked individually on activities. Learners in Rick's class recognized that he held them *responsible* for coming to class on time, actively participating during whole-class discussions and small-group work, and trying their best on assignments. Learners were given time during class to work on activities or employ the skills they were learning and seek guidance from Rick. For example, on special practice activities for the Basic Skills Test, Rick usually completed one or two with the whole class before students worked on their own or with partners. This way of organizing instruction allowed Rick time to see how students interpreted tasks and provided a forum for solving small misunderstandings or problems before they escalated. The activities and assignments were designed to be meaningful, interesting tasks. Rick worked to help students learn how to pace themselves so they could meet deadlines yet work in a relaxed, fun classroom environment. He often *modeled* for them how to take a research/writing assignment, break it down into manageable "bits," and apply strategies best suited to completing the task. Learners had *choice* within activities; this is the safety net Rick provided.

Students in Rick's classroom were *immersed* in many kinds of texts, including classic pieces of literature (*The Old Man and the Sea*), tradebooks read aloud in class (*Edgar Allen*), popular song lyrics, magazine articles with narrative stories and expository texts, skills sheets, and students' writings. This range provided students opportunities to experience various topics and types of reading for different purposes. Second, Rick *demonstrated* how texts are constructed and used by modeling fluent reading each day as he read aloud. He also *foreshadowed* events for students by helping them see how an author provides clues to help readers understand events. And he *modeled* or talked through how readers find these clues as they read. During minilessons as the class read the core text (e.g., *Of Mice and Men*) Rick also demonstrated how he constructed ideas about the motives of characters and the themes of books. Students were active participants in discussions, making *approximations* as they responded. If mistakes were made, Rick praised the effort and ensured that none of the other students made fun of the learner who tried. As Rick interacted with students, he was quick to provide *response*, bestowing praise for quality efforts but also offering specific information about what was done well, suggestions for stretching oneself further, and corrective language to quickly move a student forward in his or her learning. Thus, Rick's responses to each student's questions or comments were timely, relevant, appropriate, and nonthreatening.

Finally, let's take a moment to reexamine Rick's moral purpose and vision, presented in the opening section of Chapter 2. Specifically, Rick talked about the concept of engagement and his goals for learners—he wanted to facilitate interesting, meaningful interactions in which all students felt good about themselves as people and about their ability to learn. This vision is enacted in the classroom lesson previously presented. In the transcript we see a teacher who considers learners' sociocultural backgrounds and their cognitive and affective needs as he plans and makes moment-by-moment decisions in his classroom. Learners believed that their ideas were respected and honored and that they could and would learn in this classroom.

Rick had great insight into the students in his classroom. He developed relationships with students that enabled him to understand them as people and as learners. And he built his classroom practices on conditions of learning that would support learners as they developed their literacy knowledge and skills. In the next chapter we will continue to explore new knowledge about literacy, learners, literacy practices and events, and discourses that determine who learns and what is learned in classrooms. Before reading the next chapter, please address the questions posed in the following Reflection Point. After completing the Reflection Point activity, use the ideas in Box 5-5 to assist you as you analyze your videotaped lesson.

*Reflection Point*_____

Identify a teaching and learning activity or event in your classroom that you want to learn more about. Enlist the help of a colleague and ask him or her to videotape your lesson. Set up the camera in a corner of your classroom where you can get a panoramic view of you and your students. Position microphones around the room that feed into the camera audio jack so that you can pick up the voices of students.

After the taping session, sit down with paper and pencil. Before watching the tape, date the paper, then write a brief paragraph that describes the purpose of the lesson, the materials used, and a bit about the students (this provides context for the events that occurred).

Watch the tape in its entirety, jotting down a few notes to provide an outline of the events that occurred, but for the most part keeping your eyes on the video. Only write on two thirds of the paper, leaving one third of the paper in the right-hand margin for analysis notes.

After you finish watching the video, write down on a separate sheet of paper your initial reactions to what you saw. Take this opportunity to get out of your system all the comments about how you looked and acted and the possible "bloopers" you made.

Now, take your outline of events and expand it, watching the video a second time to ensure that you have a complete description. Note parts in the video that you want to revisit to transcribe verbatim because the interactions are interesting to you and deserve a closer analysis.

Watch the video a third time with the transcript, stopping at interesting points and writing notes in the analysis column interpreting what you think was happening and why. (See Box 5-5 for strategies to analyze the videotape.)

BOX 5-5

Analysis of the Videotape

These strategies will help you analyze and reflect on your actions and those of your students. First, look through your outline and think about what you observed when watching the video as you write down your ideas about the following:

• What are the students doing during the lesson—how are they learning?

• What evidence is there of student learning?

• What were my actions during the teaching and learning process?

• Which of my actions seem to support/not support students as they learn?

• What kind of interactions do I see between peers and between the students and me (social and academic) that support/don't support learning?

• What kinds of relationships appear to exist between students and me and between peers?

• What do I know about each individual student, both as a person and a learner?

Describe examples from the video that provide evidence for claims/responses to the bulleted items above.

Chapter 6

Understanding and Reflecting on Literacy Events and Practices

Let me tell you about what I do in my reading class. I usually get my stuff done, you know, type it on the computer and then I'll go up and get one of the CDs and I'll go back and get on a CD-ROM. And I'll start messing around, you know. Checking out the pictures and search— things like that.... I want to get on the World Wide Web—call up some people and say "Hey, what's up?" I'm going to do a report in here [this class]…we got a choice. We can also work in groups and then you read. We read four or five times in the last week—like gang related stuff— some dude shot himself. Or stuff in the newspaper or open a book and read a chapter—I mean a story out of it [anthology selection]. Or you can work on the computer and you write and stuff. I like this class. You know, a year ago all I wanted to do was stay at home, sit on the couch, and smoke cigarettes.

Mike, a student in the Jefferson High Literacy Lab

Mike is a thoughtful student who has grown up quickly. He has several step-siblings who are older than he is, and when my colleagues and I met him, he was living with his mother and father. He described his dad as a "biker" who "almost got killed." Mike is fascinated with fixing classic cars and appears to be knowledgeable and competent at what he does. In fact, he worked at a car repair shop at age 14. At the time of the study, Mike worked on cars in his spare time between school and his job at a hamburger restaurant; he also freelanced as a painter on occasion. After a difficult time when he lived on the streets for a while and got in trouble with the law, Mike spent 4 months at a juvenile home for boys. After this episode Mike decided that he wanted to stay out of trouble and get school "done." School has never been easy for him. In elementary school he moved around a lot and attended several schools where he could not get settled. Mike related that, "you'd forget a lot of stuff" from move to move. He shared that he "punched a teacher in elementary school" and was suspended; he also had several run-ins with administrators during junior high. Mike commented that he likes Jefferson High ("it is a pretty good school") and is particularly fond of study hall, art, English, and reading in the "Lit. Lab." Mike's overall goal is to attend school, try not to get into trouble, and complete the work necessary to graduate so he can go to Ivy Technical School and learn to be a mechanic.

The description of Mike, which includes portions of an academic and life history interview, tells us a little about Mike as a person and Mike as student in the literacy lab at Jefferson High School. He brings a wealth of knowledge from his community and home life to school, including sophisticated information about cars and the work life of mechanics. He also has lived and worked in many different settings, which seem to have shaped him into an adaptable yet goal-driven individual. He indicates that he knows what he wants from school and life. It is also apparent that the literacy activities he is involved in go beyond traditional schoolwork—certainly traditional remedial reading classrooms—to reading other print and nonprint forms such as information in a variety of media from the Internet and CD-ROMs, anthologies and newspapers, and writing using multiple formats such as reports generated on the computer and in groupwork. And, as students like Mike interacted and learned new information that they shared with one another, they became a "text" that was "read" by others.

David O'Brien and his co-researchers, Rebecca Springs and Dave Stith (teachers at Jefferson High School), worked for 4 years with at-risk high school students, helping them transform a traditional remedial reading lab into a technology-rich literacy lab. During class time, students worked in small groups and individually on reading and writing media-based projects. These activities provided opportunities for learners to use multimedia computer workstations and other forms of technology to create texts/products (for more background on the literacy lab see Dillon, O'Brien, Wellinski, Springs, & Stith, 1996; O'Brien, 1998; O'Brien, Dillon, Wellinski, Springs, & Stith, 1997). O'Brien and his colleagues encouraged students to use multiple forms of literacy and both print and media texts to represent their learning. Many students explored topics that were linked to "popular" media culture. What follows is an example of one learner in this classroom who drew from the world of rock music (for a more complete discussion see O'Brien, in press).

Don was a young man in the literacy lab who was very fond of music, particularly the works of Ozzy Osbourne. Don was in the class because test scores indicated that as a high school junior he was reading at the fourth-grade level. However, like many students in class, after spending time in the literacy lab, he read at a higher level. The teachers attributed this increase in test scores to the fact that students attended classes more regularly (kids who were chronically absent reported that they came to school so they could come to the literacy lab). The increase also was attributed to the fact that the students expended effort on projects and had choices in the tasks they worked on, including a balance between selecting their own reading materials and writing topics to engaging in "required" activities (e.g., skill and strategy lessons).

Early in the year the literacy lab students were asked to write a biography, and Don chose to create a multimedia presentation about Ozzy Osbourne. He read information from many sources such as *Rolling Stone* and guitar magazines and used excerpts from various texts in his report. He also scanned in pictures of Osbourne from publications and album covers and used digitized video excerpts of Music Television interviews with him. The end result was a new text form (print plus media) that documented Osbourne's music career, organized around the themes from his album titles (these covers and titles, Don proposed, chronicled the life-changing experiences of the musician). As he worked on this project, Don expanded the idea of reading and the concept of what constituted text. He did this by creating media texts that in their planning and composition were more sophisticated than traditional print texts. Different forms of literacy were required to prepare and present this multimedia text. For example, when he completed his project, Don sat in front of a computer monitor and dubbed his verbal message to fit the visual media portion of his work. He also created a video record detailing the process and content of the final project. Following is a sample text, written by Don, to accompany a scanned picture of the album cover Blizzard of Ozz:

> Since the start of Black Sabbath, Ozzy had an alcohol and drug problem. He was constantly drunk or stoned. After the release of "Blizzard of Oz" Osbourne arrived at a meeting at Columbia Records in Los Angeles. Being drunk, Ozzy was handed two doves and told to walk in and toss the doves into the air. The first dove he tossed into the air. The second, trying to crack a joke, he bit into it and chewed its head off. After that, the second Ozzy album, "Diary of a Madman," was released in 1981.

In Don's writing we see his love of music, particularly "heavy metal," and learn about his favorite musician. Don's work indicates that he enjoyed talking about the bizarre incidents associated with Osbourne, but that he also was sophisticated enough to look beyond the glamour of a rock star's life to the personal challenges and tragedies the muscian faced. As David O'Brien notes, students like Don "want to live part of their youth through music." In fact, the lives of many kids like Don revolve around so-called popular media, particularly music, and this consuming interest solidifies their cultural identity. Music is their text—it is what they read, write, and talk about. It is a powerful shared cultural text that connects and holds these kids together. As teachers we must acknowledge, although sometimes reluctantly, that shared cultural texts like music, videos, and video games are more powerful than shared print texts. Further, the stories in this book illustrate that working to motivate adolescents, yet help them learn important literacy skills and strategies so that they can be successful in life, is an ongoing challenge we face as teachers. (See Box 6-1 for information on *Adolescent Literacy: A Position Statement*, which details the complexities of addressing adolescents' literacy needs.)

Reflection Point

Describe the different ways you use literacy in your life, particularly nonprint forms of literacy. Describe the various ways literacy functions in the lives of your students.

BOX 6-1
Adolescent Literacy: A Position Statement

Adolescent Literacy: A Position Statement (1999) was developed by the International Reading Association's Commission on Adolescent Literacy. The statement recognizes the tremendous need to address the complex issues of adolescent literacy, and urges policy makers, administrators, business people, community members, parents, and educators to commit themselves to supporting adolescent literacy. The document also addresses the following questions:

1. Shouldn't adolescents already be literate?

2. Couldn't the problem be solved by preventing reading difficulties early on?

3. Why isn't appropriate literacy instruction already being provided to adolescents?

4. What can be done?

Specifically, the position statement calls for giving adolescents the resources they need for literacy growth:

• access to a wide variety of reading material that they can and want to read

• instruction that builds both the skill and desire to read increasingly complex materials

• assessment that shows them their strengths as well as their needs and that guides their teachers to design instruction that will best help them grow as readers

• expert teachers who model and provide explicit instruction in reading comprehension and study strategies across the curriculum

• reading specialists who assist individual students having difficulty learning how to read

• teachers who understand the complexities of individual adolescent readers, respect their differences, and respond to their needs

See Moore, D.W., Bean, T.W., Birdyshaw, D., & Rycik, J.A. (1999). *Adolescent literacy: A position statement.* Newark, DE: International Reading Association.

New Definitions of Literacy

Just as definitions of learning and teaching have evolved and broadened, so, too, have definitions of literacy. For example, in *The Literacy Dictionary: The Vocabulary of Reading and Writing* (1995), Richard Venezky defines *literacy* as,

> a minimal ability to read and write in a designated language, as well as a mindset or way of thinking about the use of reading and writing in every-

day life. It differs from simple reading and writing in its assumption of an understanding of the appropriate use of these abilities within a print-based society. Literacy, therefore, requires active, autonomous engagement with print and stresses the role of the individual in generating as well as receiving and assigning independent interpretations to messages.... In current usage, the term implies an interaction between social demands and individual competence. (p. 142)

Venezky's definition indicates that literacy is more than the mechanical ability to decode words or understand a written passage. It involves knowing when and how to use particular literacy knowledge in particular situations. This definition is consistent with some theories of learning, presented in Chapter 5, in which learning is defined as a social and cognitive activity in which students actively construct knowledge.

However, many researchers have argued that we must expand definitions like Venezky's. For example, Soares (1992) adds another dimension when he notes that literacy involves "ideological values and political goals" (p. 140). Likewise Scribner (1984, cited in *The Literacy Dictionary*) notes that literacy is "the power to realize one's aspirations and effect social change...."These definitions add a *critical aspect to literacy*—it is not just being able to read to understand and write and talk to communicate meaning, but it is also the ability to use literacy to critique ideas and empower ourselves to achieve our dreams and make a difference in the lives of others.

New definitions of literacy have emerged in recent years. The stories about Mike and Don, presented earlier in this chapter, shape reconceptualized definitions of literacy that include new forms of texts, interactions, and contexts. Traditionally, we have defined a text as printed text. However, viewing, for example, is a new dimension of literacy, one that takes into account the ways we make sense of technology and media. Based on the work of Derrida (1982) and others we have been challenged to reconsider the idea of a text; *texts* are now any organized network of meaning including the system of cultural signs, inscriptions, and grammars (the talk or Discourses we use in various interactions) that shape our speech and writing and can include people as texts that are read and written. Likewise, researchers such as David Bloome and Ann Eagan-Robertson (1993) have argued, "What counts as a text cannot be determined outside of the situation itself" (p. 311). This means that a text is constructed by people in a social situation or context and the individuals involved agree that what they have created is a text—a process referred to as "textualizing." Texts, then, are more than sites of information (e.g., a textbook), rather, they are ways of knowing and are cultural tools for establishing belongingness or identity (Gee, 1996). We will talk more about the concept of "identity" later in this chapter.

In their editorial "Reinventing Literacy in New Times," Allan Luke and John Elkins (1998) indicate a need for "a vision of the texts and Discourses, skills and knowledge that might be needed by our students as they enter the worlds of work and citizenship, traditional and popular culture, leisure and consumption, teaching and learning" (p. 4). The work of the New London Group (1996), in which they introduced the concept of *multiliteracies,* is similar to Luke and Elkins's message. All these researchers consider how broadened ideas about text influence how we prepare students to read and understand various texts so they learn the ever-changing language of work, power, and community, but also learn how to create a future that is personally fulfilling and successful.

Students like Mike and Don push us to think about the literacies students already use in and out of school, and the need for educators to support students so they are prepared to function in and critically analyze a world that is reshaped daily by technological innovations. This new vision of literacy requires a reconceptualization of the concept of texts that includes popular culture. For example, Don's project on Ozzy Osbourne included both print text, oral Discourse, and a variety of media texts (images and video clips). Of equal impact are the interactions and Discourses students like Don and his friends engage in as they craft these popular media texts. (I will define *Discourses* and *interaction patterns* later in this chapter.) Further, we must consider new ways to assess students' knowledge as they create and enact new genres of texts. *Genres* are spoken and written texts that have fixed elements or patterns. For example, stories have particular organizational structures or patterns that are different from those of a report. Genres are also "fixed" because they are conventional ways we use language in our culture to accomplish certain tasks and as such, we draw from a variety of genres to communicate with others. For example, we use a variation of spoken language when we talk with teaching colleagues about educational issues versus when we talk with the parents of our students. And these language patterns are different from those we use at a party with friends or an informal gathering with family members. Further, the genres we use are always evolving because we create new ways of using language, borrowing on or blending features from those patterns we already know to fit new goals we construct or situations we encounter (Pappas, Kiefer, & Levstik, 1995). It is important to note that this definition of *genre* is different than literary genres such as fiction, nonfiction, poetry, folk literature, and pictorial forms (and subcategories within these major groups).

Finally, Elliot Eisner's (1994) notion of multiple literacies is useful as we think about new definitions of literacy and ways to assess learners' knowledge. The concept of *multiple literacies* includes the idea that people can encode and decode meaning using many different ways or forms of representation in our culture to convey or express meaning. Eisner's definition reminds us that we should not privilege print and numeracy literacies, but honor and embrace the use of art, drama, music, and other forms of representing knowledge. Let me share an example of the use of symbols and drama in Joe Ruhl's biology class as a form of literacy to explain science concepts.

In late September the students were studying the structure of DNA. This was a difficult concept for them, so Joe developed an activity to help. He asked several students to come to the front of the class and physically move around with a paper label identifying their role (e.g., molecule) as they built DNA. The rest of the class participated as well, helping the volunteers by calling out directions.

Ruhl: Excellent! Excellent! All right, a phosphate molecule and a white sugar molecule and an orange thiamin (the students form into the molecule making an "L" shape). Now the thing about these three molecules is that they like to hang out together—they like to be clumped. They travel around like this (Ruhl dramatizes the action of the molecules by moving about the student volunteers) and there's this strong force of attraction between the phosphate and the sugar called a covalent bond or bonding, and so they stay in a group of three like this (he bumps into the students who are helping him simulate the demonstration— they laugh as does the rest of the class. Joe looks around the room and notices Heidi with her nose scrunched up, exhibiting confusion. He moves to the board and continues the demonstration with magnets that have labels on them, manipulating them and providing the explanation in a different way). OK, now in pairs I want you to work together on this next activity—these are your nucleotides right here (pieces of paper to manipulate). (Students begin working, a few raise their hands; Joe walks around the room helping out). Ah ha, we have a start—wait, I'm glad those enzymes aren't working in my cells! (He teases the two students about their formation and then helps them adjust their model).

Joe asked students to use drama as a way of learning and assessing understanding in his science classroom, particularly when concepts presented in typical textbook formats were difficult to understand. The structure of DNA came alive for students and many of them were able to explain the concepts using this form of literacy instead of traditional written or verbal explanations. The discussion of the concepts and writing about them came after the support provided by a new literacy.

Examples of Eisner's multiple literacies surround us daily, but we typically find them in out-of-school contexts. For example, my family planned a special tribute to my grandmother on her 90th birthday. We drew from multiple literacies to share our message. The tribute was an expression of our admiration for my grandmother's accomplishments and her love of life and family. We wrote letters detailing special memories that we organized in a scrapbook and read to her, and we arranged a musical/dramatic performance for church. We linked together the texts of several pieces of music, wrote an introduction for the performance that one of us read aloud, and we performed the composition. Several grandchildren sang, others played musical instruments, and one great-grandson gave a dramatic interpretation of the words of one of the songs we sang. As this event unfolded, we knew it was unusual for the context of a small-town church, but the message was authentic and powerful. It was the right vehicle to communicate our thoughts and feelings, and it was a meaningful experience for the listeners as well as those who presented. As we continue on in this chapter, think about how we might draw from the concept of new and multiple literacies, including the many genres we use to accomplish various purposes in our lives, as we seek to expand our ideas about what and how students learn in school.

*Reflection Point*_____

What literacies do students currently engage in and display in your classroom?
Brainstorm ways that students could use new and multiple literacies to learn in your classroom. How might you assess this learning?

Literacy Events, Practices, and Discourses

Throughout this book I have promoted the idea that literacy or multiple literacies are socially constructed activities that occur in, and are influenced by, multiple contexts (peers groups, home and school environments). Barton (1994) relates that the social aspects of literacy could best be described in terms of the literacy practices that people draw from in literacy events. Specifically, *literacy events* are acts or occasions that involve the reading, writing, speaking, or performing of various texts. Literacy acts or occasions occur in specific contexts, including social, cultural, historical, and institutional influences, and involve individuals who are using literacy to achieve specific purposes relative to those contexts (Barton, 1994). For example, in some literacy events the purpose is learning (e.g., small-group work to complete a study guide in biology class), but for most events this is not the case (e.g., a debate over what to order your child off the children's menu at a restaurant).

Barton notes that *literacy practices* are the general cultural ways of using literacy that people draw from in a literacy event (e.g., engaging in a discussion over a book or reading the newspaper at the kitchen table each morning). In school, students typically engage in recitation sessions in which they raise their hands and take turns offering comments based on the teacher's questions. These practices are common patterns in using multiple forms of literacy in particular situations in which we bring our cultural knowledge to bear to determine who does what, when it is said and where, along with the associated ways of talking and writing. Literacy practices also have a social history, meaning that current practices are based on previous interactions. An example of a literacy event and practices that differ from common recitation patterns are evident in the excerpt from Rick Umpleby's classroom presented in the previous chapter.

Literacy practices are constructed as people interact using various *Discourses* or as sociolinguist James Gee (1996) relates, "ways of thinking, feeling, believing, valuing, and acting" (p. 313). People use Discourses to identify themselves with particular social groups and to also position themselves and others within or outside of groups. Think for a moment about the Discourses that you engage in with various groups of people. Is there one way you interact with you parents? Another way with your close friends? A different Discourse that you use in the classroom with students?

Finally, in thinking about literacy events and practices and the Discourses we use during these events, it is useful to understand learners as individuals with multiple and shifting *identities*. For example, in a case study of a student named Carolyn in Joe Ruhl's biology classroom (Dillon & Moje, 1998), I wanted to document how Carolyn was not only a student but also a daughter, a friend, and a learner who wanted to be perceived as smart. In addition, she was a young woman who sought interest from and acceptance by boys. These multiple and shifting identities are understood by thinking about how people *position themselves*—the way they act and interact with others—and the ways they are *positioned by others* during interactions—the ways they act based on the messages they get from others and society in general. For example, some students may engage in aggressive behaviors like bullying other peers because they what to create a "tough kid" image. They think this identity will make them more popular. They often are positioned by their peers and society to think that tough guys are cool (e.g., television characters in action shows). What we see is that learners' multiple identities are both created in and through their social and academic Discourses or ways of feeling, believing, valuing, and acting (Gee, 1990). (See Box 6-2 for Resources on positioning and Discourses.)

There is a need to examine and reflect on interactions among peers and between teachers and learners to see how individuals position them-

BOX 6-2
Resources for Learning More About
Positioning and Discourses

Dillon, D.R., & Moje, E.B. (1998). Listening to the talk of adolescent girls: Lessons about literacy, school, and life. In D.E. Alvermann, K.A. Hinchman, D.W. Moore, S.F. Phelps, & D.R. Waff (Eds.), *Reconceptualizing the literacies in adolescents' lives* (pp. 193–223). Mahwah, NJ: Erlbaum.

Gee, J.P., & Crawford, V.M. (1998). Two kinds of teenagers: Language, identity, and social class. In D.E. Alvermann, K.A. Hinchman, D.W. Moore, S.F. Phelps, & D.R. Waff (Eds.), *Reconceptualizing the literacies in adolescents' lives* (pp. 225–245). Mahwah, NJ: Erlbaum.

Moje, E.B., Dillon, D.R., & O'Brien, D.G. (2000). Re-examining the roles of the learner, the text, and the context in secondary literacy. *Journal of Educational Research, 93*(3), 165–180.

selves and are positioned by others during literacy events, because this positioning often determines what is learned, the way students learn, and who learns. Second, it is important to critically examine and reflect on the Discourses we use and promote in our classrooms and those that our students use to determine the extent to which individual learners are empowered or disempowered by these Discourses. In the next section of this chapter I will examine literacy events, practices and Discourses in more detail. But first, take a few moments to write and reflect about your own literacy practices, Discourses, and identities.

Reflection Point

What are some of your multiple and shifting identities? Describe how you position yourself as a person? A teacher? A community member? How do others (or how does society in general) position you, possibly influencing you to construct a new identity?

Understanding Literacy Events and Practices: Part 1

Carolyn was a tenth-grade student in a biology class at Jefferson High School who I met several years ago when I spent a year in her classroom. Labeled as average in ability, Carolyn, a White student from a middle-class background, had many goals for her academic and personal life as she entered high school. She told me about her goals and her thoughts about school and teachers one day during lunch:

> This is a bigger school and there's more people to meet, more social activities.... I like socializing with people. Last year I didn't learn that much. When I got bad grades I had to stay home and study two hours every night. Then I'd have to do what I normally do [chores around the house]. Then I could go out… then I'm free. School is important to me and it's important to my parents…[they're] divorced and they're both remarried. I'm presently living with my mom.
>
> My goal [in biology] is to get good grades because I want to get into a good college for veterinary studies…. However, I'm not keen on work that much but when I have to do it, I'll do it. I have to study or I don't understand stuff. I've been on the honor roll until I got into high school. Then my grades slipped the first semester. I had a different teacher for biology last semester and my grade wasn't that good. I didn't learn that much. I was just bored half out of my mind. But I like stuff this semester with Mr. Ruhl [my teacher]. Our class is fun and interesting. Our teacher makes us do our labs and everything right. We work in study groups and we can have four different conversations going and still get work done. I really like group work.

What does this vignette tell us about Carolyn the daughter? The student? The young woman? From listening to Carolyn we learn about her family and responsibilities at home. We see her fears about a new school with lots of students, yet she expresses excitement about meeting new people. We become aware of her dream of becoming a veterinarian, yet see her struggles with learning biology content. She also described teachers and classes that supported her learning, as compared to those that did not. I will focus on Carolyn as we examine two literacy events, closely observing her as she interacts with others and working to understand how various practices and Discourses support or detract from her learning. In the following Reflection Point we will examine the first literacy event involving Carolyn and her group members discussing the sheep liver fluke.

Reflection Point

Reread the transcript from Chapter 2, focusing primarily on Carolyn. Write a description of what happens in the small group. What do the interaction patterns look like—who talks, when do they talk, and what do they talk about? What multiple forms of literacy are students engaged in? Take a closer look at the interactions and analyze the Discourse or "ways of thinking, feeling, believing, valuing, and acting" that you see that denotes this particular social group. How does Carolyn position herself as a member of the group? How was Carolyn positioned by others?

After completing this Reflection Point, I invite you to compare your analysis with mine. First, I describe what is going on. Then I focus my analysis on Carolyn.

Description. The students are struggling to understand the idea of how the liver fluke cycle operates. In general, most of the students participate in the interactions, freely offering comments and "trying out" ideas without fear of ridicule from peers. At one point they appear to get off topic, discussing school lunch programs; they joke about what they are served, and what they will or will not eat. Eventually, they return to the task with Carolyn drawing a picture to represent her ideas about the cycle (a cow with waste emerging from underneath its tail).

Analysis of interactions and Discourse patterns. When we look closely at Carolyn, we see that she positions herself to be a key player in the groupwork. First, she was the only girl in the group at this time. The boys often deferred to her because they liked her and were a bit in awe of her. In this position, Carolyn was a key player in the interactions, feeling free to question ideas or the responses given by group members that she believed were not adequate. However, she rarely used her power in the group to disempower others. What you could not see during this interaction was Carolyn's use of her body to position herself with peers. She leaned forward to talk, giggled at jokes, reached over to grab someone's arm or punched them to gain their attention. She often giggled and ran her fingers through or flipped her hair. These messages were often in conflict with the message she also transmitted—that of competent group member. Carolyn's goal appeared to be to position herself in a way in which she contributed to the work of the group but she was also able to have fun, socialize, and entertain her peers as they worked together.

When students were asked to talk about their work in this group, most agreed that everyone chipped in and did his or her part and that they liked the idea of working in a group in which they felt comfortable with one another; they also liked the idea of equal membership in the group with no leader. Although it appears that group members cut in on Carolyn's responses or interrupted her from time to time, this type of cutting in and tagging on to comments was a common characteristic of all members of this group. It appeared that there was respect for Carolyn when she questioned her peers: "I think we need more than that" because the group continued to struggle with ideas as opposed to writing down an incomplete answer. Interestingly, when asked in interviews, some members of the group stated that Carolyn was a contributing member. Others, like Jay, noted that she often got the group off task and liked to have fun during class. Nevertheless, Jay always wanted to work with her.

If we judge Carolyn's interactions and abilities by this analysis alone, or if we only see glimpses of her actions within this lesson and make judgments about her as a student, we might conclude that she focused on fun over academics—that she was off task. In fact, Carolyn was positioned this way by Joe Ruhl, who observed her "off-task" actions (giggling, talking about school lunches, flipping her hair) from afar as he traveled around the room, looking up occasionally as he worked with several groups. The multiple demands we as teachers assume, particularly when dealing with groupwork and the needs of individual students, influences how we see students and may promote the inadvertent positioning of students like Carolyn. Using a critical lens we could also ask whether issues such as Carolyn's gender, class, and academic abilities also influenced how teachers viewed her actions and Discourses. What we know from interviews is that Joe saw her as less interested in academics than she actually was. He also did not have Carolyn's life and school history data to draw from; these data, which were added later, would have made him aware of Carolyn's goal to become a veterinarian. Further, having the opportunity to examine the liver fluke lesson transcript, life history data, and Carolyn's actions in groupwork over time might have allowed Joe to see something different in her Discourses and actions in one lesson.

Understanding Literacy Events and Practices: Part 2

Carolyn appeared to learn a lot and succeed in biology class (based on assignments and test grades) and enjoyed the unspoken power and sense of equality in the groupwork presented in Chapter 2. However, she longed to interact with students who were more popular in her class because she wanted to position herself as popular and smart. Thus, when Joe re-organized the groups and put her in a setting where she could interact with Mike, she was initially very pleased. Mike was perceived by Carolyn to be cute, popular, and smart. In reality his work indicated an average level of achievement but his previous group consisted of several top students in class. Thus, Joe Ruhl, Mike, and others in the class assumed that if Mike worked with the smartest students, he must be one of the smartest students. And the fact that Joe asked Mike to lead one of the new groups was another indicator to Mike that he was being given the "power" associated with group leader. With the advent of a group leader, the interaction patterns changed and Discourses shifted dramatically for Carolyn and others in the group.

As the group leader, Mike's goal was to move the group along as they completed the study guide. The literacy practice of "struggling" between group members was replaced with the leader assuming the primary role within the group. Interaction patterns typically included Mike reading the study guide questions, Mike finding the answers in the textbook or asking Mr. Ruhl, and Mike verbally dictating what everyone should write on their guides. As leader Mike used various Discourses, including verbal and nonverbal cues, to assume power and control of the interactions and Discourses of others. What follows is a description of Mike and Carolyn's group, presented in three segments to allow analysis of each segment before moving on to the next. I encourage you to analyze the data with me, writing descriptive notes about what you see occurring, analyzing and interpreting what you see, and reflecting on how the Discourses and subject positions assumed or assigned affect who learns, how learning occurs, and how students feel about their experiences.

As the group of students (Joey, Carolyn, Jeff D., Tracy, & Mike G.) formed, Mike positioned himself as leader and opened his book. The students had their study guides open and looked at the first question: What are pheromones? Mike and Carolyn were sitting next to each other on one side of the table. Carolyn leaned close to Mike, shy in her attempts to gain his attention but occasionally grabbing his arm to do so. With her head resting in her hand, and with a flip of her hair, she moved her study guide toward Mike.

Mike:	(to Carolyn) You already have it don't ya? [the study guide filled out]
Jeff:	Pher...mone... (struggling with the pronunciation)
Mike:	What? What are "phermone" [sic]...chemical? (reading off guide and book—the textbook has *pheromone* [FEHR-uh-mohn])
Carolyn:	There we go.
Jeff:	Thanks.
Jeff:	(reading aloud from the textbook) "...that affects the behavior of the species."
Mike:	(reading out of the book and writing as he dictates) "Phermones [sic] of species."
Carolyn:	I already got all that guys.
Jeff:	You do?
Carolyn:	Uh huh.
Jeff:	(to Carolyn) When did you do that [complete the study guide]?
Mike:	What'd you do, work ahead? (goes on to the next question on the study guide and reads it aloud). "How do they [insects] use it [pheromones]?" To communicate with other organisms and...(he pulls over Carolyn's study guide and copies from it)

Analysis of group discussion. In this dialogue we learn that Carolyn came to the group session with her study guide already filled out. This action defeats the purpose Joe set up for students to struggle in group-work. But this new group did not have a history of working together.

Carolyn's intent was to offer her study guide to Mike as a way of positioning herself as smart. Carolyn seemed to know that her actions would allow Mike to easily have the answers he needed to assume his role as group leader. She also knew that if the group had the answers they could save time so that they could socialize as they worked. Carolyn also may have completed the guide prior to the group session because she often wanted the time outside of class to think about the questions and her responses. She did not feel comfortable taking risks with members of this group yet, especially Mike, whom she sought to impress. At this point in the lesson, Carolyn occupied a position of confident student and young woman. But being competent placed Carolyn in a bind: If she appeared to be too competent, she might overshadow the group leader, Mike, and lose favor in his eyes. In the next segment notice Carolyn's interactions and Discourses and I will try to describe her nonverbals and that of another group member. Notice the actions of another group member, Jeff, as well. He was a newcomer to the school and this class yet his peers had already positioned him as a person with low social and academic status.

Mike:	Wait a minute—like what is that? (He tries to read Carolyn's writing where she gives an example of a pheromone) "some wink"?
Carolyn:	Wait a minute, wait a minute! (Trying to read her own study guide which Mike now has)
Mike:	What's that—What's that—"wink"?
Carolyn:	Like somebody winks at you?
Jeff:	Yeah, but that's not really from the pharomoon [sic].
Joey:	Why not?
Jeff:	Because. It's an action.
Joey:	So?
Carolyn:	So?

Mike looks at both male group members then raises his hand to get the teacher's attention.

Joey:	"Sending those waves" is an action too.
Mike:	Is that true? (Looking at Ruhl for confirmation)
Carolyn:	(mimicking) Is that true?
Mike:	(to Joe Ruhl) Do you think that humans use phermones [sic] or whatever [however you pronounce that word]?

Jeff:	Pharmones [sic].
Mike:	Yeah.
Ruhl:	Pheromones?
Joey:	Yeah, like somebody winks at ya.
Ruhl:	Yeah, pheromones—all right, if somebody winks at you that's a message.
Joey:	Wouldn't that be the same thing?
Ruhl:	Well in the sense that pheromones carry messages, but pheromones are scents—they're chemicals, they're smells.
Mike:	Yeah. Wild.
Ruhl:	Diffused through the air…
Carolyn:	Perfume. Perfume.
Ruhl:	OK (to Carolyn) it might be an artificial pheromone but it's a chemical that carries a message.
Mike:	Yeah, have you heard anybody say, "Yeah, you smell real good," then they start floating. I saw that in the movies.
Jeff:	You actually pay attention to the movies?
Carolyn:	(laughs) geez Mike, he pays attention to the movies even if his girlfriend's sitting there.
Mike:	She can stay home for all I care—I don't have one. (He reads aloud from Carolyn's guide) "Fertilization and delment [sic] [development] of eggs."
Jeff:	Hold it. (Mike never looks up—Jeff hands Mike his completed study guide to copy from. Mike takes it but doesn't look at it.)
Jeff:	Yeah, the development of eggs. Yeah, yeah, it's all right here (pointing to his guide).

Analysis of group discussion. In this segment there is a small conflict over Carolyn's answer of "wink" as an example of pheromone. Mike, positioning himself as the leader, does not turn to his peers to talk through other options but immediately seeks out Ruhl—the "leader for group leaders." In fact he ignores Jeff and Joey as they attempt to question a response and struggle to understand the concept of pheromones. Carolyn, who offered the answer of "wink," is momentarily taken off guard when she is positioned by her peers as having less than credible answers.

However, she regains her academic and social position when she offers "perfume" as an answer that gains partial approval from Ruhl. As a result, Carolyn gains approval from Mike. There is some flirting and an exchange of personal information between Mike and Carolyn (Mike makes it clear that he does not have a girlfriend) although the whole group is privy to this information. Throughout these interactions, Mike remains in control of the group, rejecting Jeff's answers (Jeff also came with the study guide partially filled out, perhaps because he had witnessed how this helped Carolyn connect with Mike). Mike also monitors his power as a group leader by comparing the progress of his group to others. When he sees that his group is behind, he becomes a taskmaster, chastising his group for being behind, telling them to be quiet, get serious, and quit slacking off. He becomes more dictatorial in his Discourse. In the next segment, we will examine how Mike positioned Carolyn into a new and disempowered identity. This resulted from a discussion of a book read in particular high school English classes (academic versus general track), and the academic status associated with reading some texts over others.

Carolyn:	What's this book about anyway, guys? (looking at a paperback copy of *Les Miserables*)
Mike:	What'd you put? (Looks at Jeff but then continues to write)
Jeff:	(answering Carolyn) I haven't the slightest idea [what the book is about].
Joey:	You're not reading it [the book] in English?
Carolyn:	Uh uh [no].
Mike:	(to Carolyn) Who do you have [as a teacher]? (He continues writing as he talks.)
Jeff:	I have it [the book] but I'm not reading it.
Carolyn:	(laughs)
Joey:	(to Carolyn) Aren't you taking English 1?
Carolyn:	Uh huh [yes]. (her response seems hesitant, uneasy)
Mike:	No you're not.
Carolyn:	Uh huh [yes]. (now a bit embarrassed)
Mike:	No you're not. You got to read this book or you can't pass [English 1].
Jeff:	Aren't you taking...
Mike:	English 2?

Jeff:	…academic English?
Carolyn:	(quietly, softly) No, I'm in general. (She looks at Jeff.)
Jeff:	You are? (incredulously)
Mike:	OK, then that explains it. (He continues writing.)
Tracy:	(to Mike) I don't get it—what's the disadvantage of parthenogenesis? (Tracy isn't involved in this side conversation and appears to just be focused on getting her study guide filled out.)
Joey:	(to Carolyn) OK, so Math 3 but general English instead.
Mike:	Yeah, we're taking academic. (to Tracy) What? (He turns the study guide to the next page to catch up with Tracy and answer her question.)
Tracy:	(answers her own question) No sex life.
Jeff:	Yeah, Yeah, Yeah…
Carolyn:	If he calls me stupid I'll hit him.
Jeff:	I'm not going to call you stupid. Before I left [my former school] I didn't read that but I read a novel and I don't feel like reading again.
Joey:	That's stupid but that's your privilege.
Mike:	(still talking to Tracy) I know what's happening(?)
Tracy:	Is that [answer] right? I think it's…. What'd you put for #6 (she looks at Jeff now)?
Mike:	I didn't [get an answer to that one].
Mike:	(looks around at the group) No sex life [is the answer].
Jeff:	I'm gabbing.
Carolyn:	What? What sex life? (She turns to join the group).
Mike:	Yours, none? Mine is different. (He begins reading aloud from the study guide page.) "The social insects are the most advanced, most complex of all the invertebrate animals if you want to know about these social insects…."
Carolyn:	No sex. (laughs—as she leans over to read Mike's answers on his study guide)
Mike:	I said I was direct, man! If you don't know it….

Analysis of group discussion. In this segment the Discourses of group members and one of the written texts used by the group (paperback read in English class) shaped a new identity for Carolyn—one in which she did not contribute academically or socially within the group. For all practical purposes she was silenced for the rest of the literacy event. How did this happen? The turning point for Carolyn occurred when she asked group members about the paperback novel. Her question made it evident to all that she was not in a class where it was being read. Mike was quick to make everyone aware that all academic track students had to read this particular book. Probably the most disempowering actions were Mike's relentless attempts to make Carolyn admit she was not in an academic track English class, including his statement "Oh, that explains it." These Discourses, along with the comment "We're taking academic" were Mike's way of reaffirming his position as leader within the group and repositioning Carolyn as a "less than credible" group member.

Meanwhile Jeff and Joey attempted to help Carolyn reposition herself. In fact, these two group members could not believe that Carolyn was in a lower track English class. Based on their history with Carolyn in biology class, particularly their experiences with her in a different group context where a "struggling" Discourse was apparent, they had come to believe in her knowledge and abilities and they valued her as a peer. Jeff employed self-deprecation as a way of helping Carolyn reposition herself into her former identity.

Meanwhile, Carolyn became defensive, believing that everyone thought she was stupid. She eventually regained her composure but decided that joking around and flirting were the only viable ways to positively reposition herself socially with Mike (as opposed to working with him on the academic tasks in groupwork). She commented to him in a half flirting, half teasing way "What, no sex life?" and he replied with "Yours—none." Carolyn deferred to Mike on all counts, erasing her answers on her study guide and leaning over the lab table to copy what he wrote and dictated. She did not participate in the academic Discourse of the group except to ask for answers or laugh at Mike's jokes. She seemed to relinquish her academic and social identities to Mike, assuming a position of giggling girl with few ideas about biology, who must depend on the male group leader.

As a postscript, Mike rejoined his original group a few weeks later. When I talked to him about this decision he said that he left the group with Carolyn and others because they were "slackers" (that is, he was having to do all the work for the group). He characterized his peers as "always talking and goofing off" and he did not like being behind the other groups in terms of the speed and amount of work they completed each day compared to this new group. When Mike departed from the group the rest of the members ranged in emotion from being relieved, to embarrassed, to a bit aggravated. Most attempted to reorganize into their former groups. Carolyn reconstituted her old group and added a few new members. Within a day she had shifted back to her previous identities of academic and social leader in a group in which no one student was the leader. The group continued to work together the rest of the semester with all members achieving average or better than average end-of-the-semester grades. (For more complete information about Joe Ruhl and his students, see Dillon & Moje, 1998 and Dillon, O'Brien, & Volkmann, in press.)

Reflecting on Our Own Practices: A Strategy

We can gain a great deal of insight about students as individuals and how they learn by watching, listening, and seeking to understand literacy events, practices, and Discourses enacted in our classroom. First, we can see that literacy learning is embedded in and shaped by the social and cultural values, beliefs, and knowledge shared by a group of people. Also, students use multiple literacies to indicate what they know. Literacy events like groupwork look different from class to class, group to group, and person to person. The literacy practices or the ways of using literacy that students draw from are based on their previous interactions, yet they are also constructed on a moment-by-moment basis by learners as they interact together. These practices may not match our visions of what learning should look like. And often there are discrepancies for students between previous and new practices (e.g., "struggling" in one group and a "leader" in another group).

For these reasons, it is important to examine practices and Discourses in our classrooms and other contexts. We need to understand the multiple identities our students shift in and out of, the positions they seek to assume, and those they are encouraged or forced to occupy or those they are kept from. We also need to understand how learners make sense of literacy practices and events in and out of school, and how this knowledge affects their lives and what they learn. And as my colleague, Elizabeth

Moje, and I have noted elsewhere, we as teachers need to use a critical lens to examine our practices and those of our students to see ways that we support (or ways we inadvertently deter) students as they seek to create new and powerful identities. Questions we might ask ourselves include the following (adapted from Dillon & Moje, 1998, pp. 221–222):

- How can I listen to learners more carefully and critically? How might I use videotapes, interviews, and observations to better see, hear, and understand students' experiences?

- How might my allegiance to particulars ways I like to teach or routines I like to follow limit my ability to see or hear learners' needs?

- How might my curriculum exclude the interests of and questions posed by learners?

- How can I help students position themselves in ways in which they have voice and power during literacy events and thus are able to learn in meaningful ways?

These questions will allow us to continue to examine and challenge our practices and beliefs in ways that will enable us to move toward better meeting the needs of all learners in our classrooms. Before moving on to the final chapter, please address the questions posed in the following Reflection Point.

Reflection Point

Think about a student you've worked with who has positioned himself or herself or was positioned by others. Why did the positioning occur as it did?

Videotape a literacy event in your classroom. Analyze the tape using strategies outlined in Chapter 5 (see Box 5-5 and the Reflection Point prior to this box). What literacy practices are evident? Describe the Discourse patterns and how they shape individuals' actions and the event.

Examine your responses to these questions. How do students' identities influence your thoughts about them as learners and your interactions with them during lessons?

Chapter 7

A Postscript on Insight

I just finished reading Patricia MacLachlan's book, Through Grandpa's Eyes. *In this book MacLachlan tells the story of a little boy who spends a lot of time at his favorite house—his Grandpa's—because he has learned to see this house through his Grandpa's eyes. The little boy relates, "Grandpa is blind. He doesn't see the house the way I do. He has his own way of seeing." We learn that Grandpa "sees" that it is morning when the warmth of the sun touches him. He sees where grandma is by closing his eyes and listening for the familiar sounds of pots and pans banging in the kitchen. And he sees what food will be served for breakfast by discerning smells, many of which are blended together. The little boy shares that his grandpa learns to play new cello music by listening instead of reading notes, and he knows that the boy needs a haircut by touching his head as he puts him to bed. Grandpa can even see that grandma is smiling despite her firm reprimand at bedtime to "go to sleep." The story closes with the little boy reflecting about the new things he has learned by looking at the world through his Grandpa's eyes.*

Deborah Dillon

My primary goal in writing this book was to challenge myself and other educators to focus on individual students as persons and as learners—to keep kids in sight as we engage in teaching and learning practices. In Chapter 1 I defined insight and provided examples of insightful teaching. In Chapter 2 I discussed how developing insight requires a sense of where we are headed and how to get there. Where you are headed is your "end in view" or what you want teaching and learning to look like or the practices in your classroom. I also talked about moral purpose and vision; the role of inquiry, reflection, and writing in achieving our moral purpose and vision; and the characteristics of responsive, planful teachers. In Chapter 3 I discussed how insight requires an understanding of where we've come from and a recognition of our students' backgrounds. I explored why it is important to write about and reflect on our literacy histories as a way to understand our cultural backgrounds, past experiences, and the individuals who helped to shape our current beliefs about literacy teaching and learning. Likewise, it is important to understand the cultural backgrounds and literacy histories of our students, the knowledges from home that they bring to school, and how we can build on this knowledge as we seek to meet students' literacy needs. In Chapter 4 I discussed how insight requires identifying our beliefs and knowledge, uncovering tensions, and solving problems that arise daily in our classrooms. I presented tensions identified by teachers and how they grappled with these issues. I explained why problems can be "our friends" and how a critical perspective of literacy is a useful way to struggle with tensions. In Chapter 5 I discussed how insight requires reconsidering the conditions of learning we set up in our classrooms and relationships we build with students. I presented findings from the research in motivation and engagement and tools to use to glean information about students' in- and out-of-school literacy practices, their interests, and who they are as people. I also discussed current research on teaching and learning. Finally, in Chapter 6 I discussed how insight requires new definitions of literacy, specifically the idea of multiple literacies. Insight also requires a close examination of literacy events and practices in our classrooms; the relationships and interactions between peers and between teachers and students; and how Discourses shape literacy events and practices and are shaped by literacy events and practices.

Just as the boy in *Through Grandpa's Eyes* learned about a new way of seeing, in this book we explored a new way of seeing the world of teaching and learning. Specifically, when we place our students in the foreground, we are more capable of gleaning insights about who they are, what they know, how they learn, and what we can do to support their efforts. Gleaning insights about learners requires new strategies for thinking about how to craft relationships and environments that support and allow learners to develop as thoughtful, critical persons. Keeping kids in sight also requires new ways of looking closely at the texture of multiple literacies, literacy events and practices, interactions and Discourses, and students' desired or assigned identities—subtleties of classroom life that often remain hidden beneath the surface of routine daily activities. And making progress toward responsive teaching requires an understanding of our own backgrounds and beliefs and an examination of the tensions we encounter when our ideas are at odds with new knowledge, or are out-of-sync with our practices.

I hope that by reading and completing the Reflection Points throughout this book that you have developed new insights to add to those that you already had about your students. I would like to conclude this book, the foundation to the Kids InSight series, by offering some ideas for how you might put together the complex ideas we have already explored and consider future directions. First, I invite you to respond to this final Reflection Point. The questions posed will allow you to pull together the ideas and writings you've engaged in across the various chapters. Your synthesis of ideas will provide a backdrop for the next segment of this chapter.

Reflection Point_____

Look across all your responses to the Reflection Points in this book. How will you use the new insights you've gleaned about learners and the knowledge you've constructed about teaching and learning to reconsider the literacy events and practices in your classroom? What questions about learners and learning have you generated?

What goals have you set for yourself as "next steps"? Why?

What might your inquiry plan ("ready, fire, aim") look like?

_____

So Where Do We Go From Here?

There is not one "right" way to proceed from here in your professional development process. However, if you have not identified a few colleagues who are interested in joining your efforts you'll want to do so. Or if there is not a learning community in your school or district, consider creating one. Current research in staff development and school renewal efforts has established that collaborative teacher-researcher teams are critical to ongoing, sound, lasting change processes. In addition, interactions with learners, parents, and community members are helpful as educators seek to define and solve literacy problems through inquiry, writing, reflection, and action and as we work to create solutions that are crafted and embraced by a broad group of stakeholders.

As you think about your professional development efforts and how to develop insights about students, you may want to move forward in a number of dynamic, yet planful ways. A good analogy to use is Flower and Hayes's (1981, 1984) model of writing, based on the processes used by mature writers. Within this model there are intertwined activities that good writers engage in, and writing is seen as a dynamic, recursive process. For example, some writers spend more time planning their writing before they write, while others jump into the task of putting ideas on paper, revising as they learn what they know or do not know about a topic as they experiment with the writing task. In addition, good writers engage in evaluating and revising their work. They look critically at their efforts and have strategies in mind to help them revise. And mature writers who monitor themselves move easily from planning, to writing, to planning again, or on to revising. While monitoring, these writers seek to ensure that their actions make sense and that they create something meaningful for themselves and their audiences.

Drawing from this analogy, I offer the following ideas for professional development.

- Form an agreement with your colleagues that you will set aside time over a school year (or more) to meet regularly to talk about literacy issues. David O'Brien and I met with LSC colleagues for an academic year on the third Monday of each month for a 2-hour time period. This allowed us time to read, collect data, and write reflections

between meetings, and we had time set aside to dialogue and problem solve at our monthly meetings.

- Write in a reflection journal every day and share your ideas with colleagues in a writing group (or at least with one colleague). Develop the
trust and courage to critically yet constructively dialogue with others,
sharing tensions as well as successes, describing as well as reflecting.

- Share some of the ideas you generated in response to Reflection
Point questions in this book. Talk about your "end in view" for students, your moral purpose, or best practices that you want to work
toward as you seek to support the learning of all students. This may
start a conversation among your colleagues that leads to the identification of several topics or readings to explore.

- Craft a general goal or inquiry plan that you and your colleagues
agree on and that drives your future work together.

- Spend less time in your initial inquiry process "aiming" where you
want to end up and begin "firing" or gathering data from students
and examining classroom practices. Analyses of data and discussion
of what you discover about yourself and students may help you
identify tensions you want to craft into problems for inquiry. For
example, you might use a tool identified in this book (Chapters
3–6) to learn more about individual students and how they learn.

- Share your analyses and reflections with your colleagues and spec-
ulate about what your insights might mean for future action. Ex-
ploratory inquiry efforts and statements in which we articulate our
beliefs and ideas help us think about what we want to know more
about and allow us to develop credible and workable ways to glean
insights. Analyze data with your colleagues as another way to learn
about learners and your practices.

- Identify issues of interest or generate inquiry problems by reading
literacy journals and books detailing new approaches to teaching
and learning. By reading this literature you can examine inquiry
problems that other teachers have posed, the tools used to address
questions, and findings generated. This knowledge provides the
basis for critical discussions as we think about the problems we
want to study collaboratively with colleagues.

Reading the literature, dialoguing with other colleagues, and engaging in inquiry allows us to sharpen our ability to see what matters in our teaching. This recursive process allows us to hone our listening and observation skills, our ability to analyze learning situations, and the thoughtfulness we apply to writing and reflecting on actions and events and what they seem to mean. This process also helps to ensure that we do not lose sight of what is most important to us—our students.

The year 2000 is here and educators are asking, What will happen in this century? What new goals do I have as a teacher of literacy? How will I make a difference in the lives of young people? I agree with author/illustrator Mary Engelbreit (1999) who has stated in her greeting cards, calendars, and other publications that "the new millennium is here—get over it; get on with it; move along." She reminds us that it is not necessary to wait for the next innovation or the newest program or the definitive answer to the challenges facing us in literacy education. Rather, we must take a giant leap of faith and continue to grapple with the challenging but meaningful issues that face us in the field of literacy.

On the other hand, Engelbreit also reminds us to take our time, to slow down and realize that time will reveal insights. Her words ring true and help us to look to each day—despite how ordinary the events and routines may appear—as an opportunity to learn something new. A reviewer of a Pulitzer prize winning novelist Michael Cunningham's *The Hours* notes that the novel's premise—a day in the life of the main character—is key to the book's success because it focuses on the concept of "ordinary." But the reviewer continues, "no one is ordinary; no hour or day exists without ramifications; without meaning; and without epiphany" (Prichard, 1999). As teachers we can connect with Cunningham's message because the students and events in our classroom that seem ordinary are not. All contributions, comments, actions, and interactions have meaning and shape who we are and where we are headed in life. Each day is enlightening.

With the advent of the new millennium, we find ourselves desiring to make changes, renew our teaching, and help students empower themselves so they can lead rich, fulfilling lives. Each day provides a new opportunity for us to keep kids in sight. In the end, time will tell the difference we have been able to make.

An Example From My Reflection Point Journal: Darin's Story

Responses to Questions

1. Describe a student you've taught that reminds you of Chibi.

I taught a fifth grader named Darin my first year of teaching. Darin was in the lowest reading group, rarely looked at me or interacted with any of his classmates, and garnered attention by yelling out disruptive comments or engaging in socially unacceptable behavior. I remember trying every behavior modification technique I had been taught as an undergraduate to maintain some sort of control over events in reading group. Darin hated group time the most because he felt uncomfortable reading aloud in a stilted fashion in front of the other kids. None of the basal stories interested him and he never read library books or other texts of his own choosing. I became frustrated and felt that I couldn't reach Darin on a professional or personal level. He seemed to hate school and everyone associated with it. However, things changed the day I brought two white rats to school and introduced a project tied to science but unassociated with our reading curriculum. "We're going to work with the American Dairy Association and participate in a research experiment," I announced. We will feed one rat milk and dairy products and the other will not receive these foods. We'll chart the rats' growth and behavior patterns and write about our findings. We'll also read about dairy products and other health issues, rats in general, and other research projects using animals and write about what we learn." Most of the students seemed very excited and I noticed a glimmer of interest in Darin's eyes. He watched as others volunteered to feed the rats the first week. He spent time observing them and writing about them in his journal. One day he asked to hold the rats and care for them during the week. He drew pictures of the rats at work and at play and asked to go to the library in his spare time to check out books about rats. I started to see Darin in a new light. I encouraged his interest in reading about rats, and I expressed enthusiasm about his drawings and his stories. Classmates, too, recognized his interest and talents when they selected one of the names he put forward as the one for the rat who received the dairy products. And at the end of the unit—when the rats had to find a home or be transported to the zoo to "participate in the food chain process"—Darin obtained permission from his parents to adopt one of the rats.

2. What strategies have you used to help you keep individual students like Chibi "in sight" as well as gleaning insights about the various learners in your classroom?

I have tried to figure out early on what students are interested in both in and out of school. I give an interest inventory on the first day of class and have students write an autobiopoem (see Box 1-1 on page 9 for an example). I also try to talk with students informally before and after class, during breaks, and over the lunch hour to learn of their dreams, fears, likes, and dislikes. I try to read aloud books I know certain students have expressed an interest in or explore units of study that students find exciting. During each school day I try to select a couple of students to focus on. For example, during small-group interactions, I observe one group each class period and record what I learned about particular students as learners and as people. I write my observational comments in a special calendar/notebook I created (this allows me to go back and monitor students and changes in their actions and responses across time as the date is already recorded). My biggest challenge is thinking about individuals as well as the whole class when I think about and plan literacy experiences; it is also challenging to adapt plans as I teach when I pick up cues from students that my approach is not working. Part of my challenge in adapting lessons centers around my need to cover content.

Analysis Chart From My Journal

What I Seem to Be Saying	What My Thoughts Seem to Mean
Question 1:	
• Darin was in the lowest reading group; he hated group time and reading aloud.	• Students who are the hardest to teach (ability and behavior-wise) are the ones I remember across my career. I often feel that I do not meet the needs of kids who need my help during lessons.
• He was not engaged in lessons; he was disruptive and seemed to have no interests; he hated school and everyone associated with it.	• I become frustrated when kids don't get engaged and when they disrupt others—I see the problem residing in the kid and not in me or the curriculum.
• Darin got excited about the rat (dairy) project. He spent time observing, writing, and reading about rats; he took care of the rats; he began to interact constructively with peers and his teacher and I encouraged his interests.	• I remember that when Darin finally got excited about something, I sought every way possible to "keep the fire going."
• I started to see Darin in a new light; I encouraged his interest.	• My challenges in working with Darin gave me new ideas about teaching that I might not have come up with myself—the tensions I experienced as I learned to meet his needs taught me a lot about Darin, kids who have trouble reading, and myself.

Question 2:

• I try to figure out students' interests early on in the year. I use interest inventories and autobiopoems to learn about kids.

• My experience with Darin taught me to learn about kids' interests early on and use this info to co-construct curriculum with my students.

• I talk informally with students during out-of-class time.

• I have found that I learn different things about kids when I am out of the context of the classroom— out of my traditional role as teacher.

• I try to read aloud books that match students' interests. I think about students' interests when designing curriculum.

• Any time I have made an effort to connect explicitly with one or more students' interests, the learning dividends have been high.

• I try to focus on several students each day. I record what I learn from observing in a notebook.

• I am interested in using ongoing assessment to understand how individual students learn, and to document what this learning looks like. I also use what I learn to influence my teaching.

• My challenge is thinking about individuals when the whole class and the content tend to be my focal points.

• It is hard to teach, assess individual students' learning while simultaneously being responsible for the learning of 25 students; it is a challenge to teach, monitor the flow of the lesson and remember what kids say and do. It is hard to discipline myself to record information each day in a systematic fashion. Also, I am often unsure of what actions to record or how to make sense of my observations.

The Five Propositions of Accomplished Teaching

The mission of the National Board for Professional Teaching Standards (NBPTS) is to establish high and rigorous standards for what accomplished teachers should know and be able to do; to develop and operate a national, voluntary system to assess and certify teachers who meet these standards; and to advance related education reforms for the purpose of improving student learning in U.S. schools. Linked to these standards is a new generation of fair and trustworthy assessment processes that honor the complexities and demands of teaching. They focus on teacher work and the difficult issues that accomplished teachers confront on a regular basis. The NBPTS assessments for National Board Certification include having teachers construct a portfolio that represents an analysis of their classroom work and participate in exercises designed to tap the knowledge, skills, disposition and professional judgment that distinguish their practice.

The NBPTS seeks to identify and recognize teachers who effectively enhance student learning and demonstrate the high level of knowledge, skills, abilities and commitments reflected in the following five core propositions.

1. Teachers are committed to students and their learning.
Accomplished teachers are dedicated to making knowledge accessible to all students. They act on the belief that all students can learn. They treat students equitably, recognizing the individual differences that distinguish one student from another and taking account of these differences in

their practice. They adjust their practice based on observation and knowledge of their students' interests, abilities, skills, knowledge, family circumstances and peer relationships.

Accomplished teachers understand how students develop and learn. They incorporate the prevailing theories of cognition and intelligence in their practice. They are aware of the influence of context and culture on behavior. They develop students' cognitive capacity and their respect for learning. Equally important, they foster students' self-esteem, motivation, character, civic responsibility and their respect for individual, cultural, religious and racial differences.

2. Teachers know the subjects they teach and how to teach those subjects to students. Accomplished teachers have a rich understanding of the subject(s) they teach and appreciate how knowledge in their subject is created, organized, linked to other disciplines and applied to real-world settings. While faithfully representing the collective wisdom of our culture and upholding the value of disciplinary knowledge, they also develop the critical and analytical capacities of their students.

Accomplished teachers command specialized knowledge of how to convey and reveal subject matter to students. They are aware of the preconceptions and background knowledge that students typically bring to each subject and of strategies and instructional materials that can be of assistance. They understand where difficulties are likely to arise and modify their practice accordingly. Their instructional repertoire allows them to create multiple paths to the subjects they teach, and they are adept at teaching students how to pose and solve their own problems.

3. Teachers are responsible for managing and monitoring student learning. Accomplished teachers create, enrich, maintain and alter instructional settings to capture and sustain the interest of their students and to make the most effective use of time. They also are adept at engaging students and adults to assist their teaching and at enlisting their colleagues' knowledge and expertise to complement their own.

Accomplished teachers command a range of generic instructional techniques, know when each is appropriate and can implement them as needed. They are as aware of ineffectual or damaging practice as they are devoted to elegant practice.

They know how to engage groups of students to ensure a disciplined learning environment, and how to organize instruction to allow the schools' goals for students to be met. They are adept at setting norms for social interaction among students and between students and teachers. They understand how to motivate students to learn and how to maintain their interest even in the face of temporary failure.

Accomplished teachers can assess the progress of individual students as well as that of the class as a whole. They employ multiple methods for measuring student growth and understanding and can clearly explain student performance to parents.

4. *Teachers think systematically about their practice and learn from experience.* Accomplished teachers are models of educated persons, exemplifying the virtues they seek to inspire in students—curiosity, tolerance, honesty, fairness, respect for diversity and appreciation of cultural differences—and the capacities that are prerequisites for intellectual growth: the ability to reason and take multiple perspectives to be creative and take risks, and to adopt an experimental and problem-solving orientation.

Accomplished teachers draw on their knowledge of human development, subject matter and instruction, and their understanding of their students to make principled judgments about sound practice. Their decisions are not only grounded in the literature, but also in their experience. They engage in lifelong learning which they seek to encourage in their students.

Striving to strengthen their teaching, accomplished teachers critically examine their practice, seek to expand their repertoire, deepen their knowledge, sharpen their judgment and adapt their teaching to new findings, ideas and theories.

5. *Teachers are members of learning communities.* Accomplished teachers contribute to the effectiveness of the school by working collaboratively with other professionals on instructional policy, curriculum development and staff development. They can evaluate school progress and the allocation of school resources in light of their understanding of state and local educational objectives. They are knowledgeable about specialized school and community resources that can be engaged for their students' benefit, and are skilled at employing such resources as needed.

Accomplished teachers find ways to work collaboratively and creatively with parents, engaging them productively in the work of the school.

Reprinted with permission from the National Board for Professional Teaching Standards. *What Teachers Should Know and Be Able to Do,* 1994. All rights reserved.

Recommendations on Teaching Reading and Writing

RECOMMENDATIONS ON TEACHING READING

Increase	Decrease
Reading aloud to students	
Time for independent reading	Exclusive emphasis on whole-class or reading-group activities
Children's choice of their own reading materials	Teacher selection of all reading materials for individuals and groups
Exposing children to a wide and rich range of literature	Relying on selections in basal reader
Teacher modeling and discussing his/her own reading processes	Teacher keeping his/her own reading tastes and habits private
Primary instructional emphasis on comprehension	Primary instructional emphasis on reading subskills such as phonics, word analysis, syllabication

Teaching reading as a process:
   Use strategies that activate prior knowledge
   Help students make and test predictions
   Structure help during reading
   Provide after-reading applications
	Teaching reading as a single, one-step act

Social, collaborative activities with much discussion and interaction	Solitary seatwork
Grouping by interests or book choices	Grouping by reading level
Silent reading followed by discussion	Round-robin oral reading

Teaching skills in the context of whole and meaningful literature	Teaching isolated skills in phonics workbooks or drills
Writing before and after reading	Little or no chance to write
Encouraging invented spelling in children's early writings	Punishing preconventional spelling in students' early writings
Use of reading in content fields (e.g., historical novels in social studies)	Segregation of reading to reading time
Evaluation that focuses on holistic, higher order thinking processes	Evaluation focus on individual, low-level subskills
Measuring success of reading program by students' reading habits, attitudes, and comprehension	Measuring the success of the reading program only by test scores

RECOMMENDATIONS ON TEACHING WRITING

Increase	Decrease
Student ownership and responsibility by:	Teacher control of decision making
-helping students choose their own topics and goals for improvement	-teacher deciding on all writing topics
-using brief teacher-student conferences	-suggestions for improvement dictated by teacher
-teaching students to review their own progress	-learning objectives determined by teacher alone
	-instruction given as whole-class activity
Class time spent on writing whole, original pieces through:	Time spent on isolated drills on "subskills" of grammar, vocabulary, spelling, paragraphing, penmanship, etc.
-establishing real purposes for writing and students' involvement in the task	
-instruction in and support for all stages of writing process	Writing assignments given briefly, with no context or purpose, completed in one step
-prewriting, drafting, revising, editing	
Teacher modeling writing—drafting, revising, sharing —as a fellow author and as demonstration of processes	Teacher talks about writing but never writes or shares own work
Learning of grammar and mechanics in context, at the editing stage, and as items are needed	Isolated grammar lessons, given in order determined by textbook, before writing is begun
Writing for real audiences, publishing for the class and for wider communities	Assignments read only by teacher

Making the classroom a supportive setting for shared learning, using: -active exchange and valuing of students' ideas -collaborative small-group work -conferences and peer critiquing that give responsibility for improvement to authors	Devaluation of students' ideas through: -students viewed as lacking knowledge and language abilities -sense of class as competing individuals -work with fellow students viewed as cheating, disruptive
Writing across the curriculum as a tool for learning	Writing taught only during "language arts" period—i.e., infrequently
Constructive and efficient evaluation that involves: -brief informal oral responses as students work -thorough grading of just a few of student-selected, polished pieces -focus on a few errors at a time -cumulative view of growth and self-evaluation -encouragement of risk taking and honest expression	Evaluation as negative burden for teacher and student by: -marking all papers heavily for all errors, making teacher a bottleneck -teacher editing paper, and only after completed, rather than student making improvements -grading seen as punitive, focused on errors, not growth

Reprinted by permission of Steven Zemelman, Harvey Daniels and Arthur Hyde: *Best Practice: New Standards for Teaching and Learning in America's Schools* (Heinemann, A division of Reed Elsevier Inc., Portsmouth, NH, 1998).

Appendix D

IRA/NCTE Standards for the English Language Arts

The vision guiding these standards is that all students must have the opportunities and resources to develop the language skills they need to pursue life's goals and to participate fully as informed, productive members of society. These standards assume that literacy growth begins before children enter school as they experience and experiment with literacy activities—reading and writing and associating spoken words with their graphic representations. Recognizing this fact, these standards encourage the development of curriculum and instruction and make productive use of the emerging literacy abilities that children bring to school. Furthermore, the standards provide ample room for the innovation and creativity essential to teaching and learning. They are not prescriptions for particular curriculum or instruction.

Although we present these standards as a list, we want to emphasize that they are not distinct and separable; they are in fact, interrelated and should be considered as a whole.

1. Students read a wide range of print and nonprint texts to build an understanding of texts, of themselves, and of the cultures of the United States and the world; to acquire new information; to respond to the needs and demands of society and the workplace; and for personal fulfillment. Among these texts are fiction and nonfiction, classic and contemporary works.

2. Students read a wide range of literature from many periods in many genres to build an understanding of the many dimensions (e.g., philosophical, ethical, aesthetic) of human experience.

3. Students apply a wide range of strategies to comprehend, interpret, evaluate, and appreciate texts. They draw on their prior experience, their interactions with other readers and writers, their knowledge of word meaning and of other texts, their word identification strategies, and their understanding of textual features (e.g., sound-letter correspondence, sentence structure, context, graphics).

4. Students adjust their use of spoken, written, and visual language (e.g., conventions, style, vocabulary) to communicate effectively with a variety of audiences and for different purposes.

5. Students employ a wide range of strategies as they write and use different writing process elements appropriately to communicate with different audiences for a variety of purposes.

6. Students apply knowledge of language structure, language conventions (e.g., spelling and punctuation), media techniques, figurative language, and genre to create, critique, and discuss print and nonprint texts.

7. Students conduct research on issues and interests by generating ideas and questions, and by posing problems. They gather, evaluate, and synthesize data from a variety of sources (e.g., print and nonprint texts, artifacts, people) to communicate their discoveries in ways that suit their purpose and audience.

8. Students use a variety of technological and informational resources (e.g., libraries, databases, computer networks, video) to gather and synthesize information and to create and communicate knowledge.

9. Students develop an understanding of and respect for diversity in language use, patterns, and dialects across cultures, ethnic groups, geographic regions, and social roles.

10. Students whose first language is not English make use of their first language to develop competency in the English language arts and to develop understanding of content across the curriculum.

11. Students participate as knowledgeable, reflective, creative, and critical members of a variety of literacy communities.

12. Students use spoken, written, and visual language to accomplish their own purposes (e.g., for learning, enjoyment, persuasion, and the exchange of information).

From International Reading Association & National Council of Teachers of English. (1996). *Standards for the English language arts*. Newark, DE: International Reading Association; Urbana, IL: National Council of Teachers of English.

Principles of Effective Teaching of Reading

Effective teachers of reading...

1. **create a community of learners in their classrooms**
   —responsibility, opportunities, engagement, demonstration, risk-taking, instruction, response, choice, time, assessment

2. **use instructional approaches based on how children learn**
   —Four learning theories: constructivist, interactive, sociolinguistic, reader response
   —teachers incorporate reading aloud, shared reading and writing, interactive writing, guided reading and writing, and independent reading and writing; during guided reading teachers and students engage in before, during, and after reading activities; teachers use a combination of reading and writing workshop approaches and literature focus units

3. **support students' use of the four cueing systems**
   —cueing systems include phonological, syntactic, semantic, and pragmatic

4. **integrate the four language arts in teaching reading**
   —talking
   —listening
   —reading (shared, guided, independent, buddy, reading aloud)
   —writing (informal writing to explore what they are learning and the writing process to explore what they have learned)

5. **view reading and writing as related processes and teach students to use them**

—reading: preparing to read, reading, responding, exploring, extending

—writing: prewriting, drafting, revising, editing, publishing

Shanahan's (1988) research identified seven instructional principles for relating reading and writing:

1. Teachers provide daily opportunities for students to read literature and write in response to their reading.

2. Teachers introduce reading and writing in kindergarten and provide opportunities for students to read and write for genuine purposes.

3. Teachers understand that students' reading and writing reflect the developmental nature of the reading and writing relationship.

4. Teachers make the reading-writing connection explicit to students by providing opportunities for them to share their writing with classmates, publish their own books, and learn about authors.

5. Teachers emphasize that the quality of the reading and writing products students produce depends on the processes they have used. For example, as student reread and talk about literature they clarify interpretations, and they revise their writing to communicate more effectively.

6. Teachers emphasize the communicative functions of reading and writing and involve students in reading and writing for genuine communication purposes.

7. Teachers teach reading and writing in meaningful contexts with literature.

6. **use good literature (poems, stories, informational books) to teach reading**

—literature published as trade books or contained in published reading programs

7. **balance direct (explicit) instruction of skills and strategies with authentic reading and writing experiences**

—children use skills automatically such as sounding out an unfamiliar word when reading or capitalizing the first letter of a name when writing

—children use strategies as problem-solving procedures—these are chosen by students and used consciously like fix-up strategies when reading and determining that the passage didn't make sense; writers use clustering to organize ideas before writing

—researchers recommend a whole-to-part organization to teaching skills and strategies. For example, students read and respond to a piece of literature (whole) then teachers focus on a skill or strategy and teach a minilesson using examples from the piece of literature (part) then students return to the literature to use what they have learned by doing more reading or writing or doing a project (whole again)

—worksheets and practice sheets are not recommended except, perhaps as extra practice

—a variety of grouping practices are used for both skill and strategy instruction; whole class, small groups, partners, and individual assignments; assignment to small groups should be flexible

8. **help students become fluent, strategic readers**

—goal of reading is comprehension and in order for students to focus on strategies and making meaning they must be fluent readers capable of identifying words automatically. Thus both decoding and comprehension are necessary for reading.

9. **use reading and writing as tools for learning across the curriculum (e.g., learning logs)**

—three benefits students gain from studying across the curriculum are the following:

   a. Students understand and remember better when they are reading and writing to explore what they are learning.

   b. Students' literacy learning is reinforced when they read and write about what they are learning.

   c. Students learn best through active involvement, collaborative projects, and interaction with classmates, the teacher, and the world.

10. **use a variety of authentic assessment procedures to plan for and document student learning**

—motivation and beliefs surveys

—running records; miscue analysis

—cloze procedure

—story retellings

—audiotapes, videotapes of reports/activities

—puppet shows, dramatizations, demonstrations

—story maps

—lists and checklists of reading and writing behaviors and strategies

—portfolios of writing and reading processes (drafts) and products

—teachers observe students and write anecdotal notes

—teachers keep lists of skills and strategies taught in minilessons

—records of reading and writing conferences

—teachers' analyses of students' invented spelling and spelling errors

—students' assessment of their own reading and writing work

Adapted From Tompkins, G.E. (1997). *Literacy for the 21st century: A balanced approach.* Columbus, OH: Merrill.

The principles listed above are drawn from research conducted over the past 25 years focused on how children learn to read and write and best practices in the elementary school. A balanced approach is promoted with high-quality literature at the core.

Learning to Read:
Core Understandings

1. Reading is a construction of meaning from text. It is an active, cognitive, and affective process.
2. Background knowledge and prior experience are critical to the reading process.
3. Social interaction is essential in learning to read.
4. Reading and writing develop together.
5. Reading involves complex thinking.
6. Environments rich in literacy experiences, resources, and models facilitate reading development.
7. Engagement in the reading task is key in successfully learning to read.
8. Children's understandings of print are not the same as adults' understandings.
9. Children develop phonemic awareness and knowledge of phonics through a variety of literacy opportunities, models, and demonstrations.
10. Children learn successful reading strategies in the context of real reading.
11. Children learn best when teachers employ a variety of strategies to model and demonstrate reading knowledge, strategy, and skills.
12. Children need the opportunity to read, read, read.
13. Monitoring the development of reading processes is vital to student success.

From Braunger, J., & Lewis, J.P. (1997) *Building a knowledge base in reading*. Portland, OR: Northwest Regional Educational Laboratory; Urbana, IL: National Council of Teachers of English; Newark, DE: International Reading Association.

References

Allen, J., Michalove, B., Shockley, B, & West, M. (1991)."I'm really worried about Joseph": Reducing the risks of literacy learning. *The Reading Teacher, 44,* 458–472.

Au, K.H. (1993). *Literacy instruction in multicultural settings.* New York: Harcourt Brace.

Au, K.H. (1998). Constructivist approaches, phonics, and the literacy learning of students of diverse backgrounds. In T. Shanahan & F.V. Rodriguez-Brown (Eds.), *Forty-seventh Yearbook of the National Reading Conference* (pp. 1–21). Chicago: National Reading Conference.

Au, K.H., & Kawakami, A.J. (1995). Research currents: Talk story and learning to read. *Language Arts, 62,* 406–411.

Au, K.H., & Mason, J.M. (1983). Cultural congruence in classroom participation structures: Achieving a balance of rights. *Discourse Processes, 6,* 145–167.

Avery, C. (1993). *...And with a light touch: Learning about reading, writing, and teaching with first graders.* Portsmouth, NH: Heinemann.

Bandura, A. (1986). *Social foundations of thought and action: A social cognitive theory.* Englewood Cliffs, NJ: Prentice Hall.

Barrentine, S.J. (Ed.). (1999). *Reading assessment: Principles and practices for elementary teachers.* Newark, DE: International Reading Association.

Barton, D. (1994). *Literacy: An introduction to the ecology of written language.* Oxford, UK: Blackwell.

Bean, T.W. (1998). Teacher literacy histories and adolescent voices: Changing content-area classrooms. In D.E. Alvermann, K.A. Hinchman, D.W. Moore, S.F. Phelps, & D.R. Waff (Eds.), *Reconceptualizing the literacies in adolescents' lives* (pp. 149–170). Mahwah, NJ: Erlbaum.

Bissex, G.L., & Bullock, R.H. (1987). *Seeing for ourselves: Case-study research by teachers of writing.* Portsmouth, NH: Heinemann.

Bloome, D., & Eagan-Robertson, A. (1993). The social construction of intertexuality in classroom reading and writing lessons. *Reading Research Quarterly, 28,* 304–333.

Boisvert, R.D. (1998). *John Dewey: Rethinking our time.* Albany, NY: State University of New York.

Braunger, J., & Lewis, J.P. (1997). *Building a knowledge base in reading.* Portland, OR: Northwest Regional Education Laboratory; Urbana, IL: National Council of Teachers of English; Newark, DE: International Reading Association.

Britzman, D.P. (1991). *Practice makes practice: A critical study of learning to teach.* Albany, NY: State University of New York Press.

Cairney, T.H. (1995). *Pathways to literacy.* London: Cassell.

Calkins, L.M. (1994). *The art of teaching writing* (2nd ed.). Portsmouth, NH: Heinemann.

Cambourne, B. (1995). Toward an educationally relevant theory of literacy learning: Twenty years of inquiry. *The Reading Teacher, 49,* 182–190.

Chaskin, R.J., & Rauner, D.M. (1995). Youth and caring: An introduction. *Phi Delta Kappan, 76,* 667–674.

Clift, R.T., Houston, R.W., & Pugach, M.C. (Eds.). (1990). *Encouraging reflective practice in education: An analysis of issues and programs.* New York: Teachers College Press.

de la Luz Reyes, M. (1992). Challenging venerable assumptions: Literacy instruction for linguistically different students. *Harvard Educational Review, 62,* 427–446.

Delpit, L.D. (1986). Skills and other dilemmas of a progressive black educator. *Harvard Educational Review, 56,* 379–385.

Delpit, L.D. (1988). The silenced dialogue: Power and pedagogy in education other people's children. *Harvard Educational Review, 58,* 280–298.

Delpit, L.D. (1995). *Other people's children: Cultural conflict in the classroom.* New York: New Press.

Derrida, J. (1982). *Margins of philosophy.* (A. Bass, Trans.). Brighton, MA: Harvester Press.

Dewey, J. (1981). Social inquiry. In J.J. McDermott (Ed.), *The philosophy of John Dewey* (pp. 399–420). Chicago: University of Chicago Press. (Original work published 1938)

Dillon, D.R. (1989). Showing them that I want them to learn and that I care about who they are: A microethnography of the social organization of a secondary low-track English-reading classroom. *American Educational Research Journal, 26,* 227–259.

Dillon, D.R., & Moje, E.B. (1998). Listening to the talk of adolescent girls: Lessons about literacy, school, and life. In D.E. Alvermann, K.A. Hinchman, D.W. Moore, S.F. Phelps, & D.R. Waff (Eds.), *Reconceptualizing the literacies in adolescents' lives* (pp. 193–223). Mahwah, NJ: Erlbaum.

Dillon, D.R., O'Brien, D.G., & Volkmann, M. (in press). Reading and writing to get work done in high school biology. In E.B. Moje & D.G. O'Brien (Eds.), *Constructions of literacy: Studies of teaching and learning in and out of secondary schools.* Mahwah, NJ: Erlbaum.

Dillon, D.R., O'Brien, D.G., Wellinski, S.A., Springs, R., & Stith, D. (1996). Engaging "at-risk" high school students: The creation of an innovative program. In D.J. Leu, C.K. Kinzer, & K.A. Hinchman (Eds.), *Literacies for the 21st century: Research and practice* (Forty-fifth Yearbook of the National Reading Conference (pp. 232–244). Chicago: National Reading Conference.

Dixon-Krauss, L. (1996). *Vygotsky in the classroom: Mediated literacy instruction and assessment.* White Plains, NY: Longman

Eaker-Rich, D., & Van Galen, J. (1996). *Caring in an unjust world: Negotiating borders and barriers in schools.* New York: State University of New York Press.

Eisenhart, M.A., & Borko, H. (1993). *Designing classroom research: Themes, issues, and struggles.* Boston: Allyn & Bacon.

Eisner, E.W. (1991). *The enlightened eye: Qualitative inquiry and the enhancement of educational practice.* New York: Macmillan

Eisner, E.W. (1994). *Cognition and curriculum reconsidered* (2nd ed.). New York: Teachers College Press.

Elbow, P. (1998). *Writing without teachers.* New York: Oxford University Press.

Engelbreit, M. (1999, December 25–27). So the millennium is just around the corner—get over it; get on with it. *USA Today,* cover page.

Erickson, F., & Schultz, J. (1992). Students' experience of the curriculum. In P.W. Jackson (Ed.), *Handbook of research on curriculum: A project of the American Educational Research Association* (pp. 465–485). New York: Macmillan and the American Educational Research Association.

Ernest, P. (1989). The knowledge, beliefs and attitudes of the mathematics teacher: A model. *Journal of Education for Teaching, 15,* 13–34.

Farr, R.C., & Tone, B. (1998). *Portfolio and performance assessment: Helping students evaluate their progress as readers and writers* (2nd ed.). New York: Harcourt Brace.

Fenstermacher, G.D. (1999). Agenda for education in a democracy. In W.F. Smith & G.D. Fenstermacher (Eds.), *Leadership for educational renewal: Developing a cadre of leaders* (pp. 3–27). San Francisco, CA: Jossey-Bass.

Flower, L., & Hayes, J.R. (1981). A cognitive process theory of writing. *College Composition and Communication, 32,* 365–387.

Flower, L., & Hayes, J.R. (1984). Images, plans, and prose: The representation of meaning in writing. *Written Communication, 1,* 120–160.

Fraser, J., & Skolnick, D. (1994). *On their way: Celebrating second graders as they read and write.* Portsmouth, NH: Heinemann.

Fullan, M. (1993). *Change forces: Probing the depths of educational reform.* London: Falmer.

Galda, L., Cullinan, B.E., & Strickland, D.S. (1997). *Language, literacy, and the child* (2nd ed.). New York: Harcourt Brace

Gambrell, L.B., Palmer, B.M., Codling, R.M., & Mazzoni, S.A. (1996). Assessing motivation to read. *The Reading Teacher, 49,* 518–533.

Gee, J.P., & Crawford, V. M. (1998). Two kinds of teenagers: Language, identity, and social class. In D.E. Alvermann, K.A. Hinchman, D.W. Moore, S.F. Phelps, & D.R. Waff (Eds.), *Reconceptualizing the literacies in adolescents' lives* (pp. 225–245). Mahwah, NJ: Erlbaum.

Gee, J.P. (1990). *Social linguistics and literacies: Ideology in discourses.* London: Falmer Press.

Gee, J.P. (1996). *Social linguistics and literacies: Ideology in discourses* (2nd ed.). London: Taylor and Francis.

Glesne, C., & Peshkin, A. (1992) *Becoming qualitative researchers: An introduction.* White Plains, NY: Longman.

Goodlad, J.I., Soder, R., & Sirotnik, K.A. (Eds.). (1990). *The moral dimensions of teaching*. San Francisco, CA: Jossey-Bass.

Graham, R.J. (1991). *Reading and writing the self: Autobiography in education and the curriculum*. New York: Teachers College Press.

Gregory, E. (1995). What counts as reading: Children's views. In P. Murphy, M. Selinger, J. Bourne, & M. Briggs (Eds.), *Subject learning in the primary curriculum: Issues in English, science, and mathematics* (pp. 89–101). New York: Routledge.

Guthrie, J.T., & Wigfield, A. (Eds.). (1997). *Reading engagement: Motivating readers through integrated instruction*. Newark, DE: International Reading Association.

Harp, B. (1996). *Handbook of literacy assessment and evaluation*. Norwood, MA: Christopher-Gordon.

Harris, T.L., & Hodges, R.E. (Eds.). (1995). *The literacy dictionary: The vocabulary of reading and writing*. Newark, DE: International Reading Association.

Heath, S.B. (1982). What no bedtime story means: Narrative skills at home and school. *Language and Society, 11*, 49–76.

Heath, S.B. (1983). *Ways with words: Language, life, and work in communities and classrooms*. New York: Cambridge University Press.

Hemingway, E. (1952). *The old man and the sea*. New York: Charles Scribner.

Henk, W.A., & Melnick, S.A. (1995). The Reader Self-Perception Scale (RSPS): A new tool for measuring how children feel about themselves as readers. *The Reading Teacher, 48*, 470–482.

Hernandez, H. (1990). *Multicultural education: A teacher's guide to content and process*. Columbus, OH: Merrill.

Hitchcock, G., & Hughes, D. (1992). *Research and the teacher: A qualitative introduction to school-based research*. New York: Routledge.

Hubbard, R.S., & Power, B.M. (1999). *Living the questions: A guide for teacher-researchers*. York, ME: Stenhouse.

International Reading Association & National Council of Teachers of English. (1996). *Standards for the English language arts*. Newark, DE: International Reading Association; Urbana, IL: National Council of Teachers of English.

Jackson, P. (1986). *The practice of teaching*. New York: Teachers College Press.

Jersild, A.T. (1955). *When teachers face themselves*. New York: Teachers College Press.

Johnston, P.H. (1992). *Constructive evaluation of literate activity*. White Plains, NY: Longman.

Johnston, P.H. (1997). *Knowing literacy: Constructive literacy assessment*. York, ME: Stenhouse.

Kamberelis, G., & Dillon, D.R. (1997). *Comparative literacy memoirs*. Unpublished document, Purdue University, West Lafayette, IN.

Kirby, D., Liner, T., & Vinz, R. (1981). *Inside out: Developmental strategies for teaching writing*. Montclair, NJ: Boynton/Cook.

Ladson-Billings, G. (1994). *The dreamkeepers: Successful teachers of African American children*. San Francisco, CA: Jossey-Bass.

Luke, A., & Elkins, J. (1998). Reinventing literacy in new times. *Journal of Adolescent & Adult Literacy, 42*, 4–7.

MacLachlan, P. (1980). *Through grandpa's eyes*. New York: HarperCollins.

Meyer, D.K. (1993). What is scaffolded instruction? Definitions, distinguishing features, and misnomers. In D.J. Leu & C.K. Kinzer (Eds.), *Examining central issues in literacy research, theory, and practice* (Forty-second Yearbook of the National Reading Conference, pp. 41–53). Chicago: National Reading Conference.

Moje, E.B. (2000). *"All the stories that we have": Adolescents' insights about literacy and learning in secondary schools*. Newark, DE: International Reading Association.

Moje, E.B., Dillon, D.R., & O'Brien, D.G. (2000). Re-examining the roles of the learner, the text, and the context in secondary literacy. *Journal of Educational Research, 93*, 165–180.

Moll, L. (1998). Turning to the world: Bilingual schooling, literacy, and the cultural mediation of thinking. In T. Shanahan & F.V. Rodriguez-Brown (Eds.), *The forty-seventh Yearbook of the National Reading Conference* (pp. 59–75). Chicago: National Reading Conference.

Nespor, J. (1987). The role of beliefs in the practice of teaching. *Journal of Curriculum Studies, 19*, 317–328.

Neufeld, J. (1999). *Edgar Allen*. New York: Puffin.

New London Group. (1996). A pedagogy of miltiliteracies: Designing social futures. *Harvard Educational Review, 66*, 60–92.

Nias, J., Southworth, G., & Campbell, P. (1992). *Whole school curriculum development in the primary school*. London: Falmer Press

Nieto, S. (1999, December). *Language, literacy and culture: Intersections and implications*. Presentation at the 49th Annual Meeting of the National Reading Conference, Orlando, FL.

Nisbitt, R., & Ross, L. (1980). *Human inference: Strategies and shortcomings of social judgment*. Englewood Cliffs, NJ: Prentice-Hall.

Noddings, N. (1986). *Caring: A feminine approach to ethics and moral education*. Berkeley, CA: University of California Press.

Noddings, N. (1992). *The challenge to care in schools: An alternative approach to education*. New York: Teachers College Press.

Noddings, N., & Witherall, C. (1991). *Stories lives tell: Narrative and dialogue in education*. New York: Teachers College Press.

O'Brien, D.G., Springs, R., & Stith, D. (in press). Engaging "at-risk" high school students: Literacy learning in a high school literacy lab. In E.B. Moje & D.G. O'Brien (Eds.), *Constructions of literacy: Studies of teaching and learning in and out of secondary schools*. Mahwah, NJ: Erlbaum.

O'Brien, D.G. (1998). Multiple literacies in a high-school program for "at-risk" adolescents. In D.E. Alvermann, K.A. Hinchman, D.W. Moore, S.F. Phelps, & D.R. Waff (Eds.), *Reconceptualizing the literacies in adolescents' lives* (pp. 27–49). Mahwah, NJ: Erlbaum.

O'Brien, D.G., Dillon, D.R., Wellinski, S., Springs, R., & Stith, D. (1997). *Engaging "at-risk" high school students* (Perspectives in Reading Research Technical Report No. 12). Athens, GA: National Reading Research Center.

Olson, M.W. (1990). *Opening the door to classroom research*. Newark, DE: International Reading Association.

Pajares, M.F. (1992). Teachers' beliefs and educational research: Cleaning up a messy construct. *Review of Educational Research, 62*(13), 307–332.

Pappas, C.C., Kiefer, B.Z., & Levstik, L.S. (1995). *An integrated language perspective in the elementary school: Theory into action* (2nd ed.).White Plains, NY: Longman.

Paley,V.G. (1979). *White teacher*. Cambridge MA: Harvard University Press.

Paley,V.G. (1990). *The boy who would be a helicopter*. Cambridge MA: Harvard University Press.

Paley (1997). Foreword. In I. Hall, C. Campbell, & E.J. Miech (Eds.), *Class acts: Teachers reflect on their own classroom practice* (pp. vii-ix). Cambridge, MA: Harvard University Press.

Pennebaker, J.W. (1997). *Opening up: The healing power of expressive emotions*. New York: Guilford.

Piestrup, A.M. (1973). *Black dialect interference and accommodation of reading instruction in first grade* (Monographs of the Language-Behavior Research Laboratory, No. 4. Berkeley, CA: University of California.

Pinnell, G.S., & Matlin, M.L. (1989). *Teachers and research: Language learning in the classroom*. Newark, DE: International Reading Association.

Pintrich, P.R., & Schunk, D.H. (1996). *Motivation in education: Theory, research, and applications*. Englewood Cliffs, NJ: Merrill.

Prichard, A. (1999, April 17). Pulitzer prize-winning novel describes ordinary life as extraordinary. *Journal & Courier Newspaper*, p. B10.

Rex, L., Green, J., Dixon, C., & the Santa Barbara Discourse Group. (1998). What counts when context counts? The uncommon "common" language of literacy research. *Journal of Literacy Research, 30*, 405–433.

Rhodes, L.K. (1993). *Literacy assessment: A handbook of instruments*. Portsmouth, NH: Heinemann.

Rhodes, L.K., & Shanklin, N. (1993). *Windows into literacy: Assessing learners, K–8*. Portsmouth, NH: Heinemann.

Rogoff, B. (1990). *Apprenticeship in thinking: Cognitive development in social context*. New York: Oxford University Press.

Rorty, R. (1982). *Consequences of pragmatism: Essays, 1972–1980*. Minneapolis, MN: University of Minnesota Press.

Rose, M. (1989). *Lives on the boundary: The struggles and achievements of America's underprepared*. New York: Penguin

Rose, M. (1995). *Possible lives: The promise of public education in America*. New York: Houghton Mifflin.

Salmon, P. (1988). *Psychology for teachers: An alternative approach*. London: Hutchinson.

Sarason, S.B. (1990). *The predictable failure of educational reform: Can we change course before it's too late?* San Francisco: Jossey-Bass.

Schmidt, P.A. (1997). *Beginning in retrospect: Writing and reading a teacher's life*. New York: Teachers College Press.

Schon, D.A. (1987). *The reflective practitioner: How professionals think in action*. San Francisco, CA: Jossey-Bass.

Schon, D.A. (Ed.). (1991). *The reflective turn: Case studies in and on educational practice*. New York: Teachers College Press.

Shannon, P. (1990). *The struggle to continue: Progressive reading instruction in the United States*. Portsmouth, NH: Heinemann.

Shore, B. (1999). *The cathedral within: Transforming your life by giving something back*. New York: Random House.

Smith, W.F., & Fenstermacher, G.D. (1999). *Leadership for educational renewal: Developing a cadre of leaders*. San Francisco: Jossey-Bass.

Soares, M.B. (1992). *Literacy assessment and its implications for statistical measurement: Current surveys and research in statistics*. Paper prepared for the Division of Statistics, UNESCO, Paris.

Spangenberg-Urbschat, K., & Pritchard, R.H. (Eds.). (1994). *Kids come in all languages: Reading instruction for ESL students*. Newark, DE: International Reading Association.

Strickland, K., & Strickland, J. (2000). *Making assessment elementary*. Portsmouth, NH: Heinemann.

Tompkins, G.E. (1997). *Literacy for the 21st century: A balanced approach*. Columbus, OH: Merrill.

Tremmel, R. (1993). Zen and the art of reflective practice in teacher education. *Harvard Education Review, 63*(1), 434–458.

Turbill, J., Butler, A., & Cambourne, B. (with Langton, G.) (1991, 1993). *Frameworks: A whole language staff development program 3–8*. Stanley, NY: Wayne Finger Lakes Board of Cooperative Services.

Turner, J.C., & Paris, S.G. (1995). How literacy tasks influence children's motivation for literacy. *The Reading Teacher, 48*, 662–673.

Vygotsky, L.S. (1978). *Mind in society: The development of higher psychological processes* (M. Cole, V. John-Steiner, S. Scribner, & E. Souberman, Eds. and Trans.). Cambridge, MA: Harvard University Press. (Original work published 1934)

Watson, D.J. (1994). Whole language: Why bother? *The Reading Teacher, 47*, 600–607.

Webster's New Collegiate Dictionary. (1979). Springfield, MA: G. & C. Merriam.

Wigfield, A. (1997). Children's motivations for reading and reading engagement. In J.T. Guthrie & A. Wigfield (Eds.), *Reading engagement: Motivating readers through integrated instruction* (pp. 14–33). Newark, DE: International Reading Association.

Witherell, C., & Noddings, N. (Eds.). (1991). *Stories lives tell: Narrative and dialogue in education*. New York: Teachers College Press.

Wolcott, H.F. (1990). *Writing up qualitative research*. London: Sage.

Wood, D., Bruner, J.S., & Ross, G. (1976). The role of tutoring in problem-solving. *Journal of Child Psychology and Psychiatry, 17*(2), 89–100.

Yashima, T. (1955). *Crow boy*. New York: Puffin/Penguin Books.

Zemelman, S., Daniels, H., & Hyde, A. (1998). *Best practice: New standards for teaching and learning in America's schools* (2nd ed.). Portsmouth, NH: Heinemann.

Zinsser, W. (Ed.). (1987). *Inventing the truth: The art and craft of memoir*. Boston: Houghton Mifflin.

Author Index

A

ALLEN, J., 11
ALVERMANN, D.E., 137
APPLE, M., 91
AU, K.H., 58, 59, 62, 65, 96, 105

B

BANDURA, A., 76, 111
BARTON, D., 136
BEAN, T.W., 49
BLOOME, D., 132
BOISVERT, R.D., 23
BRAUNGER, J., 94, 175
BRITZMAN, D.P., 49
BRUNER, J.S., 109

C

CAIRNEY, T.H., 46, 47f, 97, 108, 109, 113
CALKINS, L.M., 50
CAMBOURNE, B., 86, 113, 114, 115
CAMPBELL, P., 29
CHASKIN, R.J., 26
CRAWFORD, V.M., 137
CULLINAN, B.E., 46

D

DANIELS, H., 94, 167
DE LA LUZ REYES, M., 64, 65
DELPIT, L.D., 64, 65
DERRIDA, J., 132

D (right column)

DEWEY, J., 23, 45
DILLON, D.R., 61, 99, 100, 129, 137, 148, 149
DIXON, C., 61
DIXON-KRAUSS, L., 108

E

EAGAN-ROBERTSON, A., 132
EISNER, E.W., 16, 133, 135
ELBOW, P., 5
ELKINS, J., 132, 133
ERICKSON, F., 100
ERNEST, P., 76

F

FENSTERMACHER, G.D., 2, 23, 24
FLOWER L., 37, 154
FULLAN, M., 21, 22, 27, 30, 32, 44, 45, 82, 83

G

GALDA, L., 46
GEE, J.P., 132, 136, 137
GOODLAD, J.I., 22, 23
GRAHAM, R.J., 49
GREEN, J., 61
GUTHRIE, J.T., 110

H

HAYES, J., 37, 154

Subject Index

Note: Page reference followed by *t* or *f* indicates tables or figures, respectively.

C

D